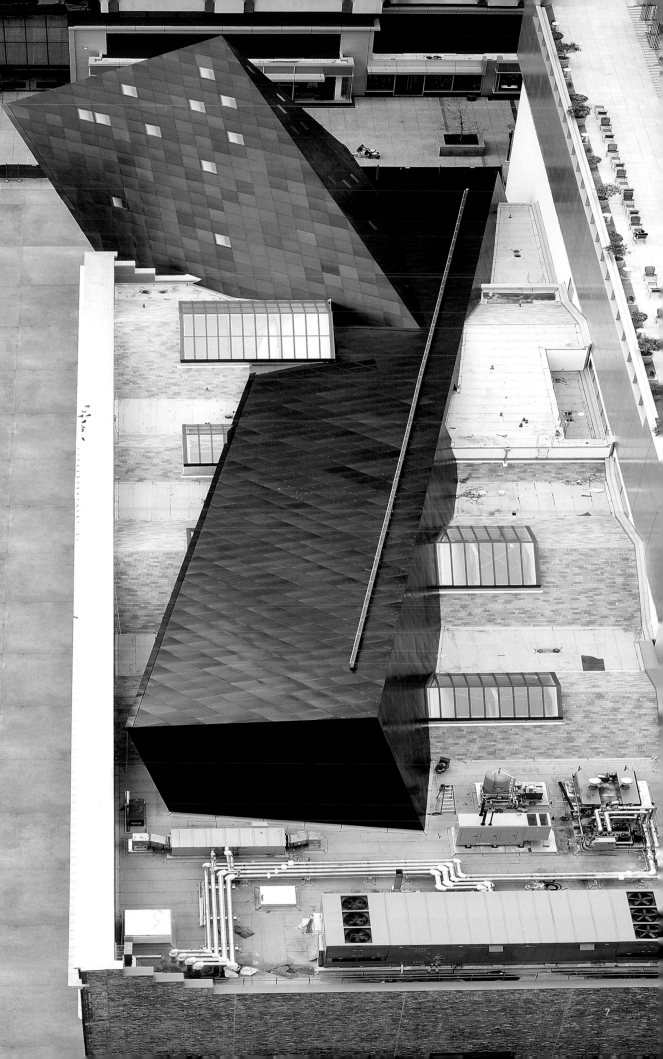

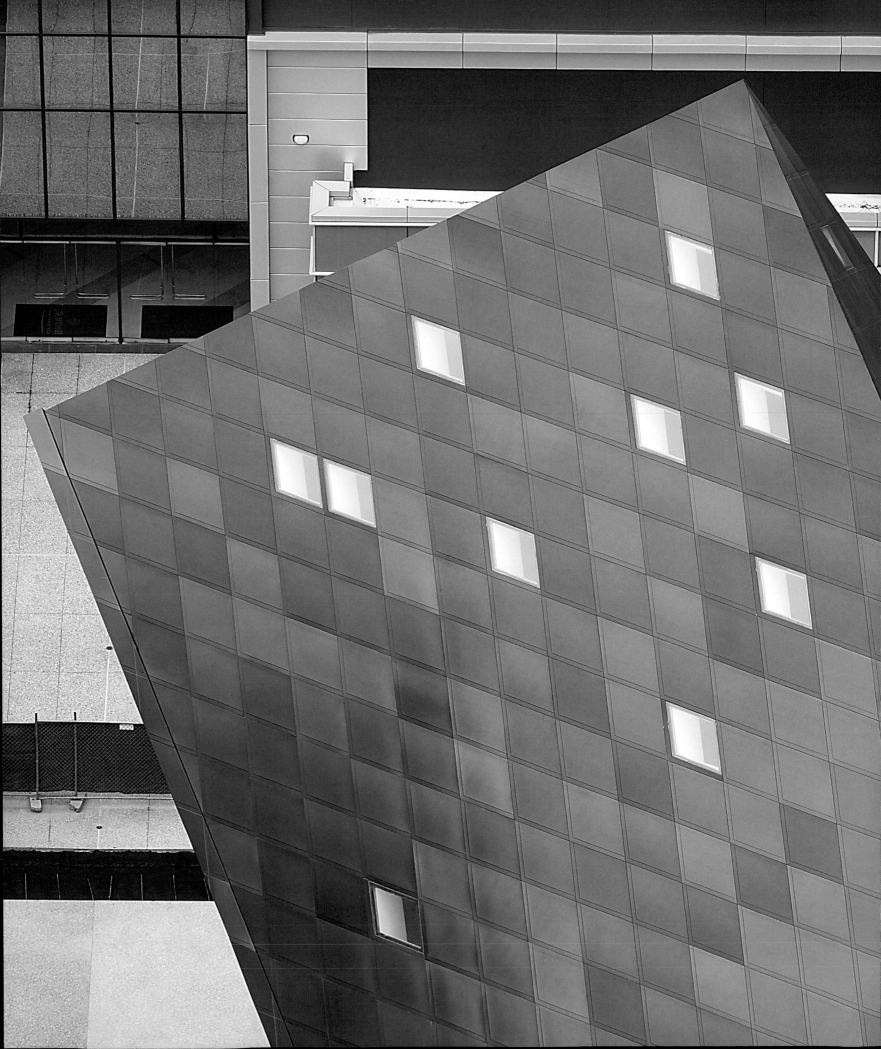

THE FABRIC
OF CULTURE
Fashion, Identity, Globalization

February 15 - April 27, 2008

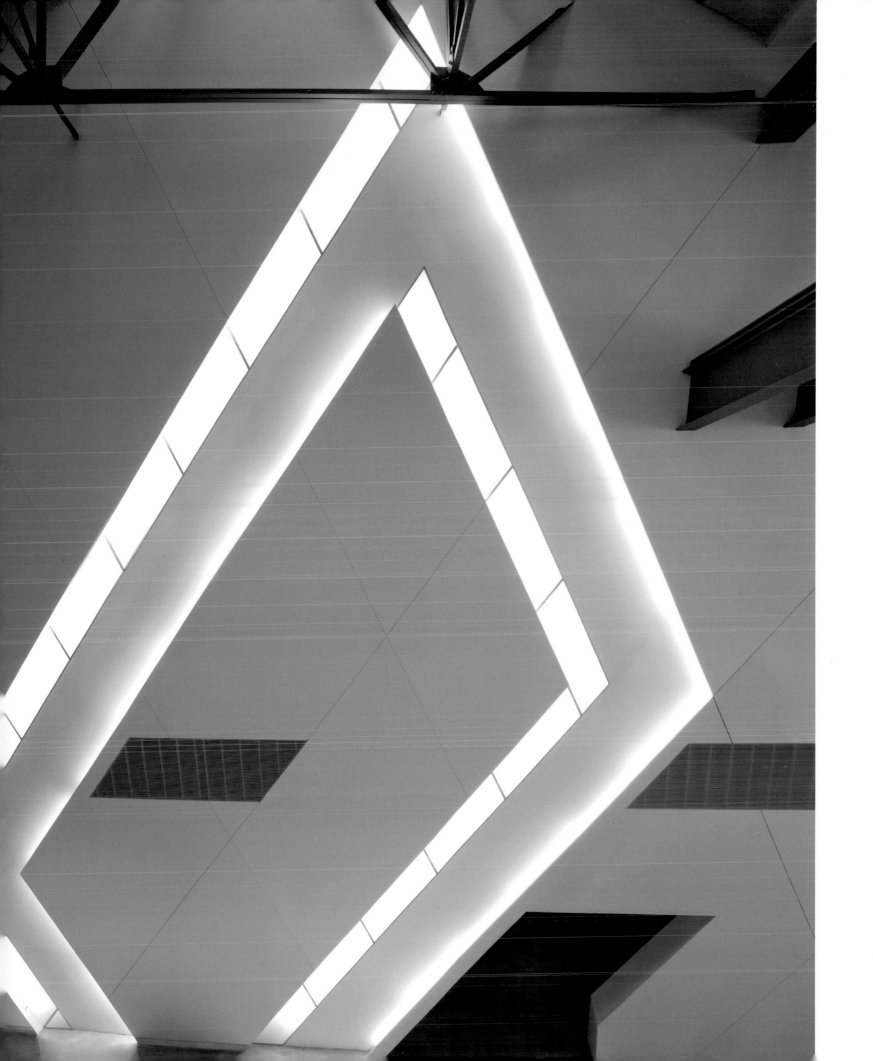

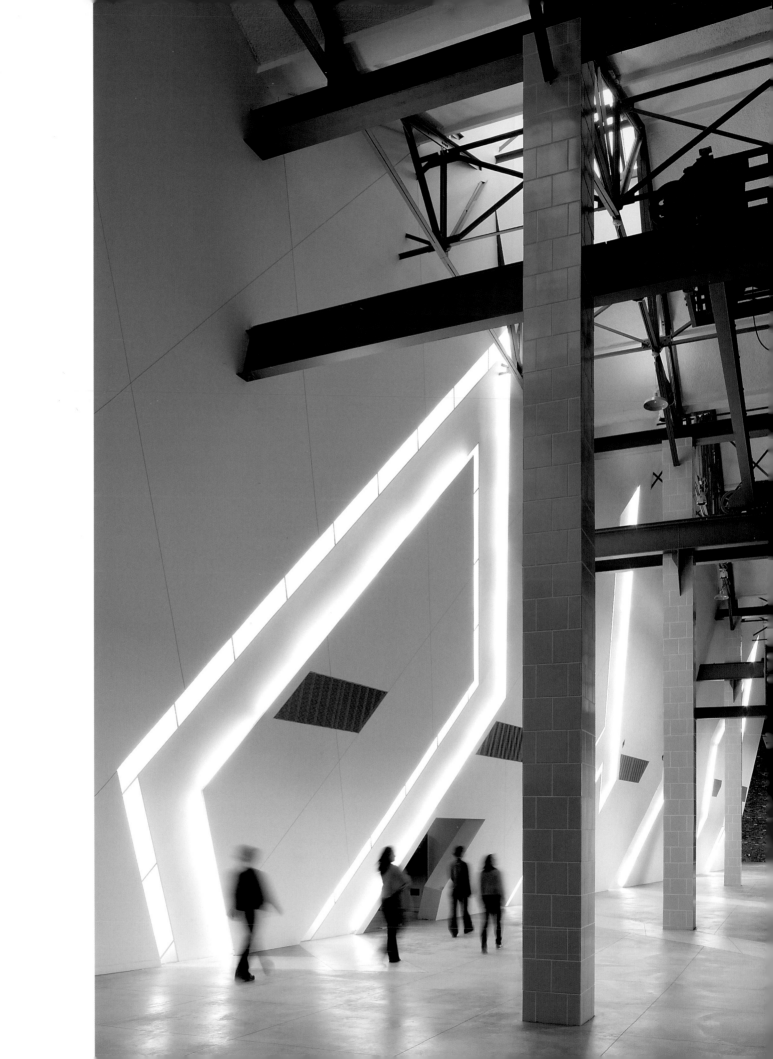

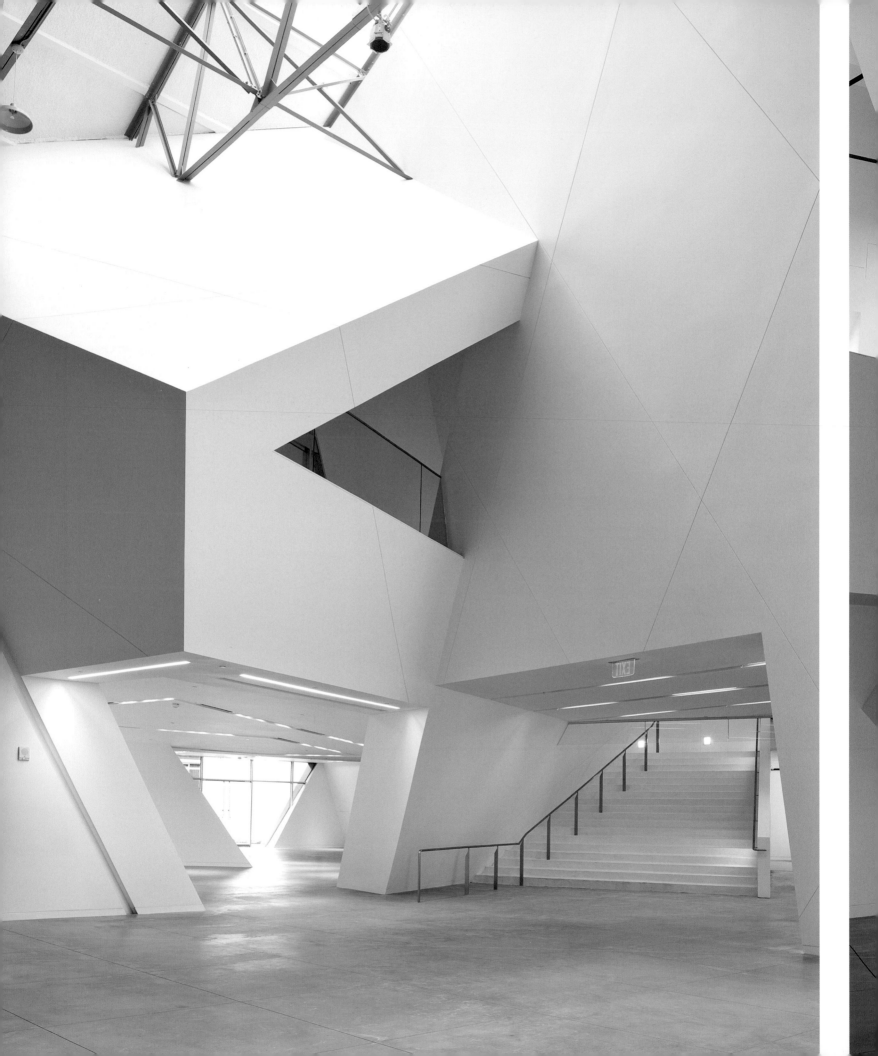

DANIEL LIBESKIND
and the CONTEMPORARY JEWISH MUSEUM:
New Jewish Architecture from Berlin to San Francisco

edited by
Connie Wolf

with contributions by
Daniel Libeskind, Mitchell Schwarzer,
and James E. Young

First published in the United States by

Rizzoli International Publications, Inc.
300 Park Avenue South
New York, New York 10010
www.rizzoliusa.com

Skira Editore S.p.A.
Palazzo Casati Stampa
Via Torino 61
20123 Milan
Italy
www.skira.net

Contemporary Jewish Museum
736 Mission Street
San Francisco, California 94103
www.thecjm.org

Library of Congress Control Number 2008926427
ISBN: 978-0-8478-3165-4

A catalogue record for this book is available
from the British Library.

The paper in this book meets the guidelines for permanence
and durability of the Committee on Production Guidelines
for Book Longevity of the Council on Library Resources.

10 9 8 7 6 5 4 3 2 1

Front jacket and front cover photography by Bruce Damonte
Back jacket and front cover photography by Bitter Bredt Fotografie

Three-quarters of a century after the first Berlin Jewish Museum opened in 1933, in the space of a mere decade we have witnessed the building of four new Jewish museums in the cities of Berlin, Osnabrück, Copenhagen, and San Francisco. Behind all of these projects is the architect Daniel Libeskind, whose vision and intelligence have brought new and challenging perspectives to the role of Jewish museums in contemporary society. As we open a new chapter in the history of the Contemporary Jewish Museum in San Francisco with the inauguration of the new building, Libeskind's first Jewish museum in North America, we pay homage to all those who have had a hand in building this institution and bringing it to maturity, and also to the many individuals who are responsible for making possible the extraordinary new building on Jessie Square. This book, published on the occasion of the opening of the new museum, celebrates the communities in Berlin, Osnabrück, Copenhagen, and San Francisco who have invited Daniel Libeskind to create Jewish museums rooted in the past and yet inspiring a new vision for the future which embraces dialogue and intercultural exchange.

While Libeskind has designed many other distinctive buildings during this period, there is no other living architect who has transformed the way we think about Jewish history and culture and its future in contemporary society in such a broad and extensive way. In each of his Jewish museum projects, Libeskind was presented with an extraordinary challenge: how to work with an existing historical structure to create a new kind of landmark, one that reflects the unique mission and visions of its local community and also addresses the universal Jewish experience. In San Francisco, the building site was the Jessie Street Power Substation, originally built by the Pacific Gas & Electric Company in 1881, remodeled and enlarged by Bay Area Architect Willis Polk after the 1906 earthquake and fire, and designated as a landmark building in 1976. As with his other projects, Libeskind's challenge for the CJM was to determine how to approach an existing historic structure and to integrate a new building into a complex urban site. The new museum building, clad in a vibrant blue steel and enveloped by the brick walls of the existing power substation, traverses the historic structure and extends beyond it as if reaching for the sky. In Berlin and Osnabrück, separate buildings with their own identity were designed to connect inventively with other historic structures on the site. And in Copenhagen, Libeskind dramatically transformed one wing of the interior of a building dating back to the end of the 16th century.

While working through the approval process in San Francisco, we were often asked: Wouldn't it have been easier if you were just given an empty lot on which to construct a new building? Despite the challenges that a landmarked structure posed in our case, despite the responsibilities that it entailed, we embraced the opportunity to participate in revitalizing the historical context of a building that fueled the rebirth of San Francisco after the 1906 earthquake. Providing contemporary perspectives on history, letting history come alive and inform the present, and recognizing that contemporary life is deeply rooted in history are values that are central to Jewish thought. And through his Jewish museum projects, Libeskind has embodied these values in designs that actively engage visitors of all ages and backgrounds. As Libeskind stated: "History does not come to an end but opens to the future; history is a dynamic ground."

As Mitchell Schwarzer observes in his insightful essay, the CJM differs from Libeskind's other Jewish museum projects, most notably for being far removed from Europe, where Jewish life was marked by an extraordinarily traumatic history. California, and San Francisco in particular, offered the possibility of adventure, exploration, and new beginnings, where hope could triumph over adversity. As a resident of the Bay Area, Schwarzer has studied at close range the unique cultural and urban environment that gave birth to the Contemporary Jewish Museum in 1984, and sets out an account of how the museum produced this new landmark in the context of decades-long redevelopment in the city's downtown. In his rich and illuminating essay, James E. Young, on the other hand, explores the issue of whether we can speak of a distinctly "Jewish architecture." He looks at Libeskind's Jewish museum projects, examining the way in which each one responds to the specificities of the communities in which it was commissioned – its history, development, challenges, and future. Young's analysis of the founding of the first Jewish museum in Berlin, which opened in 1933 on the eve of Hitler's rise to power, provides a touchstone for reflection on the contemporary perspectives of all of Libeskind's Jewish museum projects.

In Libeskind's own statements about his Jewish museums, he makes apparent the optimism that pervades each one. As the son of Holocaust survivors, he considers architecture to be one of the most powerful and affirmative symbols of hope, an enduring testament to the shared beliefs and values that can be transmitted through generations. He reminds us that architecture is built to last – that in the planning of these structures, much more is at stake than the logistical and practical aspects of building for durability and sustainability. The projects are also fundamentally about the spirit and the ideas that the buildings invoke and about the enduring meaning they represent for generations to come. In all of his Jewish museums, Libeskind's approach implies a passionate belief and investment in the future, in new ideas and human creativity. It is this belief and the power of his own imagination that ensure his buildings will withstand the inevitable vicissitudes of the political, social, and environmental kind, and reach beyond Jewish communities to dynamically galvanize broader civic and cultural exchange.

Museums are being built to regenerate themselves. Museums today represent a public discourse, a public activity, and a public attraction. They perform the considerable function of gathering a citizen's desires, emotions, and vision in a secular world. Museums are the places where people are mirrored in artifacts that testify to their existence.

Daniel Libeskind

Against the heroic legacy of the original Jewish Museum in Berlin, the Jewish community of San Francisco dedicates the new Contemporary Jewish Museum 75 years later. Its founding here and now marks yet another milestone of a most remarkable journey in which the full range of emotional and intellectual experience, from celebration to despair and destruction in 1933, to the triumph of hope in 2008, continues to be informed by memory and fueled by a collective belief in the future. Some of the principles on which the original Jewish Museum in Berlin was founded remain the same: to promote freedom of religion and expression, religious tolerance, and social justice; to establish a forum for interfaith exchange; and to create an environment where creativity and imagination become a resource and a force for change. Jewish museums around the world, through the vision, creativity, and hope of Daniel Libeskind, are bringing people together to learn from the past, to embrace the present, and to envision the future.

Connie Wolf
Director & Chief Executive Officer

Blue steel cladding, a classically ornamented brick wall – these are among the contrasts that strike the eye as one approaches Daniel Libeskind's Contemporary Jewish Museum in the emergent Yerba Buena district of San Francisco. Nowhere else in the city is the encounter between architecture's past and present so jarring, and yet so enticing. The unusual pairings of material, texture, and shape are riveting. One starts to wonder what kind of museum awaits? Crossing the threshold and entering into the expansive lobby, history, culture, and spirituality resonate in this soaring architectural space. Moving deeper into the galleries themselves, one feels reverberations between the sensuous breadth of what lies all around and the symbolic depth that it evokes. At some point, one gets the sense of what it is like to be in a Jewish space.

The inauguration of Libeskind's Contemporary Jewish Museum brings a dynamic new institution to the cityscape of San Francisco. When it was founded in 1984, the museum quietly took up residence in

TOWARD A CALIFORNIA JUDAISM

the Jewish Community Federation (JCF) office building on Steuart Street in the Financial District. Originally known as the Jewish Community Museum, later renamed the Jewish Museum San Francisco, it was a museum without collections and without any architectural identity whatsoever. Located just off the lobby of the JCF building, it occupied a mere 4,000 square feet and lacked adequate facilities for its vital public and educational programs. In due course, the museum's leadership recognized that in order to survive and thrive, it would need more generous space and a fixed identity in the urban context. In the mid-1990s, the museum had identified a site in the former seaman's and workingman's district

South of Market, where a number of cultural institutions, the Moscone Convention Center, and a spate of new hotels were springing up.

The potential site was occupied by the Pacific Gas & Electric Company's Jessie Street Power Substation, originally built in 1881, which supplied electricity to the city of San Francisco until it was deactivated in 1968. After the earthquake and fire of 1906, Willis Polk (best known for the revolutionary glass curtain wall of his 1918 Hallidie Building) was engaged to remodel and enlarge it to meet the needs of the city being rapidly rebuilt. In the tradition of the City Beautiful Movement, Polk embellished an otherwise featureless south-facing brick wall with cream-colored matte-glazed terra-cotta ornament. He added a cornice replete with dentils and egg-and-dart motifs and seven large and elaborately framed windows; one entrance was monumentalized by a gigantic arch, and the other ceremonially capped by a group of four putti bearing garlands of fruits and gourds.

Given Polk's stature as one of San Francisco's most inventive architects, and because his south facade was a splendid solution to the classical architectural problem of composing a wall, the Jessie Street Power Substation became a cause célèbre of the historic preservation community in the 1970s when part of the South of Market district that would later become known as Yerba Buena was slated for redevelopment. Wholesale demolition razed an area encompassing many city blocks on which very few structures were left standing. The Jessie Street Power Substation survived, avoiding the wrecking ball along with nearby St. Patrick's Catholic Church and a handful of other buildings. Although it was designated a landmark building and listed in the

National Register of Historic Places in 1976, it stood vacant for more than two decades before being offered to the CJM in 1995.

As planning for the Jewish Museum building got under way in 1996, the board initially commissioned a project from Peter Eisenman. A conceptual architect known for his Wexner Center for the Arts at Ohio State University, Eisenman proposed a building that would double as a passageway linking Market Street to the Yerba Buena district, and planned to mount a gigantic electronic screen atop the rear side of the power station, broadcasting images of Judaica as well as breaking news on the Middle East. A year later, in part because of controversy over Eisenman's attempt to extend his design onto the San Francisco Redevelopment Agency's plaza, he and the museum parted ways.

In 1998, Rabbi Brian Lurie, then president of the museum, led the board in awarding the commission to another Jewish architect, Daniel Libeskind. Like Eisenman, Libeskind was well known in academic circles for his experimental proposals and thought-provoking writings. Much more forcefully, though, Libeskind brought his Jewishness to the forefront of his process. With his Jewish Museum Berlin and the Felix-Nussbaum-Haus both under way at the time, his vision – part Talmudic and part Yiddishkeit – captivated the board and staff. In Libeskind's fractal forms and Hebraic symbols they discerned an identity for their new building that transcended customary notions of what a museum could look like and how it could function.

Libeskind had long been engaged with the transgression of architectural boundaries. In a 1981 essay "Symbol and Interpretation," he linked architecture to humanity's complex currents of thought, memory, and imagination. Architecture, he wrote, "seeks to explore the deeper order rooted not only in visible forms, but in the invisible and hidden sources which nourish culture itself, in its thought, art, literature, song and movement. It considers history and tradition as a body whose memories and dreams cannot be simply reconstructed. Such an approach does not wish to reduce the visible to a thought, and architecture to a mere construction."[1] This belief in the *symbolic* potential of architecture led Libeskind to banish customary geometries from his drawings. Rectilinear (or right-angled) shapes and spaces might meet most programmatic functions. They rarely shake people's souls, and he was after such stirrings. By contrast, a building with slicing, intersecting planes and volumes could potentially open the concrete world of the here and now to the abstract, spiritual dimension. Striking outside of the box with his projects for the Jewish Museum Berlin and the Felix-Nussbaum-Haus in Osnabrück, Libeskind hoped to transport architecture into the mythic realms of human existence.

On the other side of history and the globe, the project for San Francisco demanded an utterly different approach. California had a far shorter and altogether sunnier Jewish history than Germany, or for that matter, most places in the world. It was bereft of the blood libels, pogroms, ghettos, and concentration camps of the Old World. Drawn by the Gold Rush, Jews came to California in large numbers just when other peoples from around the globe were arriving. As pioneers, they prospered. Nowhere else in the world – not Babylon nor Rome nor Sepharad nor Ashkenaz – had so many Jews participated in the commercial development of a city and not been consigned to lasting second-class status. It must be said that amid the long history of worldwide Jewish persecution, San Francisco and California stand as blessed anomalies. Libeskind seized on the positive opportunity presented by the California Jewish experience. "Especially as an architect who has dealt with a lot of dark history that affected the Jews," he reflects, "I realized we could create a building that celebrated life in San Francisco, in the Bay Area, which was a life of possibilities, of beauty, of openness, really of America in its most vibrant and aspiring state."

In 1999, shortly after Libeskind began working on the project, Connie Wolf was appointed director of the Jewish Museum. It was at this point that the design process began in earnest. Between Berlin (where Libeskind's office was located) and San Francisco, discussions were held on angled versus straight walls and floors, natural light in galleries, flexible exhibition rooms, and most of all, the path that would engender a dynamic experience for visitors. "I was excited about the prospect of getting something other than a box," says Wolf, who envisioned a building that would physically embody the museum's mission of reaching out to younger people and propelling Jewish culture forward. "This was an institution that didn't fit into any particular category," she added. "It wasn't, strictly speaking, an art museum, a history museum, a Holocaust museum, or a museum of Judaica. I was interested in crossing traditional boundaries and seeing how all the museum's programs could intersect with the cultural life of the contemporary city. By hiring Daniel, we could do just that. We could go beyond renovating an old building. We could create a new kind of landmark, where old and new are always in conversation, and where the boundaries between art and

history, past and future, museum and civic space, begin to blur."

The design revealed to the public in February 2000 was ambitious, costly, and large – 110,000 square feet. Based on the Hebrew letters *chet* and *yud,* which combine to form the word *chai*, meaning "life," the building's dynamic shapes collided inside the prosaic shell of the old power substation. That encounter produced a highly complex and many-faceted structure whose great volumes rising above Polk's south facade were sheathed in golden-hued titanium. Inside, there were exhibitions spaces on four levels, two of them subterranean. By mid-2001, however, the project began to stall, largely because of the onset of economic recession, but also in response to the institutional reorganization of the museum.

In 2003, the renamed Contemporary Jewish Museum undertook a relaunch with a revised design by Libeskind, smaller (at 63,000 square feet), more crisply resolved as an expression of volumes, and easier for visitors to navigate. Public spaces were now restricted to two above-ground levels. The separate forms of the Chet and Yud and their powerful encounter resulting in the Chai were more legible in the revised design. The museum that opened to the public in June 2008 has followed the letter and spirit of the 2003 design.

One of the first things you notice about the completed building is the degree to which it is embedded within a dense urban fabric. The building occupies the center of a characteristically large South of Market city block. Its bold Chai emerges from the hollowed-out core of the old power substation. Skyscrapers ring the periphery, and part of the museum literally plunges into the side of the towering Four Seasons

Hotel. What some architects might have regarded as an awkward or marginal space became for Libeskind an opportunity to make connections and transgress the site's own limits. Early on, he revealed, "I realized that the museum could be a jewel, something very delicate yet powerful which would be seen from very unexpected perspectives: from Jesse Square, from Yerba Buena Lane, and from the windows of the towers looking down on it. The building wouldn't have just one image, but would be an intertwining."

That intertwining is powerfully legible as one approaches the museum from Jesse Square. If Polk's south facade expressed the highest aesthetic values of the City Beautiful Movement, Libeskind's gravity-defying blocks rising above it announce the emergence of a new and unpredictable presence in the fabric of the city. If in its time Polk's wall sought to mask the heavy machinery of urban infrastructure with a classicizing facade, Libeskind's building reverses that effect. The angular fractal forms – expressions of Jewish energy – reach out and upward into the surrounding city and inward to the museum's programmatic spaces. They are clad in steel panels oxidized blue as part of the production process, and custom-brushed in a crosshatch pattern by the English manufacturer Rimex.[2] The shade of blue changes, depending on the time of day or atmospheric conditions. "Out of the blue," Libeskind explains, "is the voice of G-d. It's out of nothing that creation happens."

It so happens that *yud* is the most energetic Hebrew letter. Along Yerba Buena Lane, on the west side of the museum, the dominant experience is that of the Yud suspended above the ground, similar to the way the *yud* hovers over a Hebrew word. Here, Libeskind juxtaposed the Yud with the apse of the neighboring

St. Patrick's Catholic Church. In Hebrew, the *yud* exemplifies transformation and creation. The Hebrew tetragrammaton *YHVH*, the unpronounceable name of G-d, begins with *yud*. So do the Hebrew words for Israel and Jerusalem. The *yud* is a catalyst for creation. "It's the smallest letter, a point really, it's a pointed letter, a beginning for Judaism. Seeing the Yud from outside and then entering into it, I hope people will enjoy the experience of its energy," explained Libeskind.

While one can enter the Museum Store through the Yud, the main entrance is located on Jesse Square. Passing through Polk's facade, one is immediately aware of the considerable height and volume of the historic structure, a sweep of space reaching almost 50 feet upward and about 200 feet across, from the café to the right to the store on the far left. Seconds later, the flood of light coming in through the large windows enhances this impression. Turning around, one sees that Polk's brick wall, the only feature of the original building preserved in situ, is supported on the interior by a grid of massive steel I-beams installed in 2004 to shore it up during construction. These now function as seismic bracing. The other walls of the old power substation were dismantled and later reconstructed, as were catwalks, cranes, and some sloping steel trusses. The old roofing structure was rebuilt to connect seamlessly with the angled planes of the new structure.

The I-beams provide a counterpoint to the expression of the *chai* inside the museum. Unlike the blue steel cladding on the exterior, the interior Chai is covered by white drywall. By toning down its surface, Libeskind gave greater prominence to the materials, colors, and textures of the old building: the rough red brick and the cast-iron mullions of the windows.

Across the Grand Lobby, the forceful brick wall faces the quiet white surfaces of the Chet, enlivened principally by gigantic illuminated characters spelling PaRDeS – the Hebrew word *pardes*, meaning "a garden beyond," and implying a set of paths one can take toward understanding and cultivating Judaism, and by analogy, a set of paths one can take in negotiating, learning from, and enjoying the museum.

Libeskind has long been immersed in music and mathematics, and in the Yud/Special Events Gallery of the CJM those passions reach a crescendo. If musical forms are experienced as concrete embodiments of a certain frame of mind, the musical line constantly exploding and reformulating itself, then the sensuous play of light on the surfaces of this deliriously angled chamber does something similar in architecture.[3] Just as Libeskind considers the atonal musical scores of the Viennese-born Jewish composer Arnold Schönberg to have inspired his project for the Jewish Museum Berlin, he has linked the Contemporary Jewish Museum with the work of the Jewish American composer George Gershwin: "Here, you're not looking at a solitary monument on a devastated ground, as in Berlin. Instead, you're standing in San Francisco on a ground that speaks of the continuity of different traditions and the possibility of a new Jewish future." Just as Gershwin expanded the range of his music by intertwining strains of the blues and jazz into the classical repertory, so too the Contemporary Jewish Museum strives to expand public engagement with Jewish culture by intertwining contemporary currents with older traditions and rituals. Libeskind has created a space from which to explore how Judaism may continue to do so into the future.

ENDNOTES
1 Daniel Libeskind, *Radix-Matrix: Architecture and Writings* (Münich and New York: Prestel, 1997), p. 154.
2 Jesse Hamlin, "Jewish Museum Blanketed in Blue," *San Francisco Chronicle* (May 6, 2007).
3 Daniel Libeskind, "Chamber Works: Architectural Meditations on Themes from Heraclitus" (1983), in *The Space of Encounter* (New York: Universe, 2000), p. 23.

JAMES E. YOUNG

Before reflecting on the notion of a specifically "Jewish architecture," I would ask: What makes any expression of culture "Jewish"? I would follow this question (in good Jewish fashion) with several others: Toward what end are we defining Jewish culture? Are there essentially Jewish qualities to Jewish culture? Is Jewish culture something produced mostly in relation to itself, its own traditions and texts? Or is Jewish culture necessarily constituted in the reciprocal exchange between Jewish and non-Jewish cultures? Indeed, can Jewish culture include works produced by Jews without explicit Jewish content, works inspired by Jewish texts or experiences, received by the Jewish world as Jewish texts, or codified and responded to as Jewish texts? In this vein, can Jewish culture include works produced by non-Jews for Jewish purposes, such as illuminated Hebrew manuscripts, synagogue buildings, or burial reliefs?

DANIEL LIBESKIND'S NEW JEWISH ARCHITECTURE

With these questions in mind, one could turn to specifically Jewish forms of cultural production – literature, art, photography, or architecture. Can the stories of Franz Kafka be regarded as parables for Jewish experience, as might Sigmund Freud's meditations on dreams and monotheism? Did Jewish-born artists like Barnett Newman, Philip Guston, and Mark Rothko produce "Jewish art"? Were Newman's meditations on martyrdom suggestive of "Jewishness" in his work? Did Guston's reflections on Jewish identity and catastrophe in his paintings make him a "Jewish artist"? Was Rothko's iconoclastic insistence on the abstract color field after the Holocaust a gesture toward the second commandment's prohibition of images? If so, did that give him a "Jewish sensibility"?

Would William Klein (b. 1928) be considered a Jewish photographer? What about Weegee (né Arthur Fellig, 1899–1968), Robert Capa (né Andreas Friedmann, 1913–54), or Brassaï (né Gyula Halász, 1899–1984)? Aside from its cheekiness, what are we to make of William Klein's mischievous remark that "there are two kinds of photography – Jewish photography and goyish photography. If you look at modern photography you find, on the one hand, the Weegees, the Diane Arbuses, the Robert Franks – funky photographers. And then you have people who go out in the woods. Ansel Adams, Weston. It's like black and white jazz."[1] Are William Klein's own photographs Jewish in their narrative, storytelling movement, figure to figure? Or would we consider these photographers Jewish because, in the words of art historian and critic Max Kozloff (who was also a photographer himself), they are "restless, voracious . . . give the impression of being always in transit yet never arriving."[2] Did Jews invent "street photography," as Kozloff argues, or is this an aesthetic common to all immigrants to any new land who see the street through new eyes?

Finally, back to the matter at hand: What is Jewish architecture? In its modern form, is it prophetic, iconoclastic, constitutively anticlassicizing and anti-authoritarian? Architectural theory's great advocate of rupture and fragmentation, Bruno Zevi, suggested as much when he wrote that:

Beneath the differences in the intentions [of modern architecture], the authentic reality comes to light, breaking the chains of classicistic slavery with its fetishes of dogmas, principles, rules, symmetries, assonances, harmonious accords, and repressive monumentalisms. Modern architecture, with its pulsating territorial and urban tensions, incorporates a prophetic component, at any rate, a capacity for hope. Jewish novelists often allude to prophecy as a lost value. Jewish architects, on the other hand, implement their plans with Messianic force. They cultivate their Jewishness in a reserved area. But the ideal, the Jewish fight for the emancipation of the 'other', exerts a force, even in architecture.[3]

Or is it a breaking of architecture's traditional chains in the specific context of the modern era, a century when the adequacy and viability of all cultural expression were called into doubt after World Wars I and II and the Holocaust?

The current generation of Jewish-born architects has certainly achieved an unequaled prominence in the field – along with Daniel Libeskind, Frank Gehry, Richard Meier, Peter Eisenman, Santiago Calatrava, James Ingo Freed, Eric Owen Moss, Zvi Hecker, Moshe Safdie, and Robert A. M. Stern are just a few of the best known. Citing the works of these architects, as well as midcentury figures like Erich Mendelsohn, Richard Neutra, and Louis Kahn, historian Gavriel Rosenfeld suggests that, even if there is no "monolithically Jewish style of architecture," it is still true that what he calls "Jewish concerns" have "begun to inform both the theoretical and aesthetic agendas of Jewish architects."[4]

Indeed, Rosenfeld has even suggested that the entire "deconstructivist" architectural movement itself arose from the "massive rupture in Western civilization caused by the Holocaust" and the subsequent

crisis of faith that led to a "rethinking and 'deconstructing' [of] the entire discipline of Western architecture." Here Rosenfeld elaborates: "Sharing the postmodern belief that the Holocaust's specifically modern origins require the abandonment of the 'project of modernity', Libeskind and Eisenman [in particular] . . . argue that the Nazi genocide provided compelling reason to abandon traditional architectural practice and to instead embrace an architecture of fragmentation, de-centeredness, and loss that reflected the reality of the postmodern, post-humanist, post-Holocaust world." That is, it may not just be "Jewish concerns" that have informed the work of Jewish architects, but the historical experiences of Jews in the 20th century that have begun to inform the discipline of architecture itself.

Here, in fact, I recall often being asked if Jewish architects were somehow predisposed toward articulating the memory of catastrophe in their work, in order to explain how Libeskind (originally selected to redesign the World Trade Center complex), Calatrava (designer of the new Fulton Street Transit Center abutting Ground Zero), and now Michael Arad (designer of the memorial at Ground Zero) have become the architects of record in post-9/11 Lower Manhattan. I typically answer that, while I see no direct references to Jewish catastrophe in these designs for the reconstruction of Lower Manhattan, the forms of postwar architecture have surely been inflected by an entire generation's knowledge of the Holocaust.[5] In discussing her design for what is arguably America's greatest 20th-century memorial – the Vietnam Veterans Memorial in Washington, D.C. – Maya Lin has acknowledged her debts to Sir Edwin Lutyens's Memorial to the Missing of the Somme (1932) in the northern French village of Thiepval, in Picardie, and Georges-Henri Pingusson's "Memorial to the Martyrs of the Deportation" (1962) on the Île de la Cité in Paris. Both are precursors to the "negative-form" realized so brilliantly by Lin, articulating uncompensated loss and absence through carved-out pieces of landscape, as well as by the visitor's descent downward (and inward) into memory.[6] After the Holocaust, artists and architects preoccupied with absence and irredeemable loss, a broken and irreparable world, have struggled to find an architectural vernacular that might express such breaches in civilization without mending them. Even if architecture is not a "Jewish art form" in its own right, as a discipline it has certainly been shaped by Jewish experiences and history, and by the Jewish identity of its practitioners.

It was with catastrophic timing that Berlin's first Jewish museum opened in January 1933, one week before Adolf Hitler was installed as chancellor. Housed in a series of refurbished exhibition halls at the Oranienburgerstrasse complex, which was already home to a spectacular synagogue as well as a Jewish community center and library, the Jewish Museum in Berlin opened quite deliberately in the face of the Nazis' rise to power.[7] But even here, the notion of what constituted a "Jewish museum" would become a matter of contention within the community itself. Would the museum present art on Jewish religious themes by both Jewish and non-Jewish artists, its founders asked? Or would it show anything by Jewish artists? The question of what constituted "Jewish art" was therefore broached. Indeed, right from the start, questions of "Jewishness," "Germanness," and even "European-ness" in art shown by the museum began to undercut the case for something called a "Jewish museum" in Berlin.

When the museum opened with a Max Liebermann show in 1933, the very idea of a taxonomy of religious communities and their art seemed an affront to the most assimilated of Berlin's Jews. Jewish art historian and director of the Berlin Library of Arts Curt Glaser attacked both the idea of a "Jewish Museum" in Berlin and the presumption that Liebermann's work was by dint of his Jewish birth alone somehow essentially Jewish, even though there was nothing thematically Jewish in it. Such an exhibition, Glaser wrote at the time, "leads to a split, which is totally undesirable, and from an academic point of view in no way justifiable. Liebermann, for example, is a European. He is a German, a Berlin artist. The fact that he belongs to a Jewish family is totally irrelevant with regards to the form and essence of his art."[8] Thus was an integrationist model for the Jewish Museum in Berlin first proposed and first challenged within days of the official opening.[9] Despite constant pressure from the Nazis over the next five years, the Jewish Museum in Berlin went on to mount several more exhibitions of works by Jewish German artists and their milieu. But with the advent of the Nuremberg Laws of 1935 defining "the Jew" as essentially "un-German," the Nazis effectively forbade all but Jews to visit the museum and all but Jewish artists to exhibit there. Whether assimilated to Nazi law or not, like the other Jewish institutions in the complex on Oranienburgerstrasse and throughout the Reich, the Jewish Museum in Berlin was first damaged, then plundered during the pogrom on Kristallnacht, November 9–10, 1938. Its new director, Franz Landsberger, was arrested and sent to Sachsenhausen before eventually emigrating to England and then the United States. The museum itself was dismantled, and its entire collection of art and artifacts confiscated by Nazi authorities.

After the war, some 400 paintings from the collection were eventually found in the cellars of the Reich's former Ministry for Culture on Schlüterstrasse. According to Martina Weinland and Kurt Winkler, the entire cache of paintings was seized by the Jewish Restitution Successor Organization (JRSO) and handed over to the Bezalel National Museum in Jerusalem, which eventually become the Israel Museum.[10]

In 1988, after many years of debate over where and whether to reestablish a Jewish Museum in Berlin, the Berlin Senate agreed to approve financing for a "Jewish Museum Department," which would remain administratively under the auspices of the Stadtmuseum, or Berlin Museum, housed in the Baroque Kollegienhaus on Lindenstrasse, but which would have its own, autonomous building. A prestigious international competition was announced in December 1988 for a project that would both "extend" the Berlin Museum and give the "Jewish Museum Department" its own space. According to planners, the Jewish department would be both autonomous and integrative, the difficulty being to link a museum of civic history with the altogether uncivil treatment of that city's Jews. Such questions were as daunting as they were potentially paralyzing: How to do this in a manner that would not suggest reconciliation and continuity? How to reunite Berlin and its Jewish part without suggesting a seamless rapproachement? How to show Jewish history and culture as part of German history without subsuming it altogether? How to show Jewish culture as part of and separate from German culture without recycling all the old canards of "a people apart"?

Rather than skirting such impossible questions, the planners confronted them unflinchingly in an extraordinary conceptual brief for the competition in which they literally became the heart of the design process. According to the text by Rolf Bothe (then director of the Berlin Museum) and Vera Bendt (then director of the Jewish Department of the Berlin Museum), a Jewish museum in Berlin would necessarily address three primary things: first, the Jewish religion, customs, and ritual objects; second, the history of the Jewish community in Germany, its rise and terrible destruction at the hands of the Nazis; and third, the lives and works of Jews who left their mark on the face and the history of Berlin over the centuries.[11] If in part their aim had been to reinscribe Jewish memory and the memory of the Jews' murder into Berlin's otherwise indifferent civic culture, it was also to reveal the *absence* in postwar German culture that demanded this reinscription.

Most notably, in describing the history of Berlin's Jewish community, the authors made clear that not only were the history of the city and that of its Jews inseparable from one another, but that nothing (not even this museum) could redeem the expulsion and murder of Berlin's Jews – "a fate whose terrible significance should not be lost through any form of atonement, or even through the otherwise effective healing power of time. *Nothing in Berlin's history ever changed the city more than the persecution, expulsion, and murder of its own Jewish citizens. This change worked inwardly, affecting the very heart of the city*."[12] In thus suggesting that the murder of Berlin's Jews had been the single greatest influence on the city, the planners also seemed to imply that the projected Jewish extension of the Berlin Museum might become the epicenter of Berlin's civic culture, a focal point for the city's historical self-understanding.

Guided by this conceptual brief, planners issued an open invitation to all architects of the Federal Republic of Germany in December 1988. In addition, they invited another twelve architects from outside Germany, among them the American architect, Daniel Libeskind, who was then living in Milan. Born in Lodz, in 1946, to the survivors of a Jewish Polish family largely decimated by the Holocaust, Libeskind had long wrestled with many of the brief's questions, finding them nearly insoluble at the architectural level. Trained first as a virtuoso keyboardist who came to the United States via Israel in 1960, he studied at the Cooper Union in New York under the tutelage of John Hejduk and Peter Eisenman, two of the founders and practitioners of "deconstructivist architecture." Thus, in his design for a Jewish museum in Berlin, Libeskind proposed not so much a solution to the planners' conceptual conundrum as its architectural articulation.

Of the 165 designs submitted from around the world by the time the competition closed in June 1989, Daniel Libeskind's struck the jury as the most brilliant and complex, and quite possibly just as unbuildable. It was awarded first prize and thereby became the first work of Libeskind's to be commissioned. As an example of process-architecture, according to Libeskind, this building "is always on the verge of Becoming – no longer suggestive of a final solution."[13] In its series of complex trajectories, irregular linear structures, fragments, and displacements, this building is also always on the verge of un-becoming, projecting a breaking down of architectural assumptions, conventions, and expectations. His drawings for the museum thus look more like sketches of the museum's ruins, a house whose wings have been scrambled and reshaped by the jolt of genocide, a devastated site being prepared to enshrine its broken forms. Libeskind's investigations seemed to ask: if architecture can be representative of historical meaning, can it also represent un-meaning and the search for meaning? The result is an extended building broken in several places. The void straight line running through the plan violates every space through which it passes, turning otherwise conventional rooms and halls into misshapen anomalies, some too small to hold anything, others so oblique as to estrange anything housed within them. The original design also included walls inclined at angles too sharp for hanging or installing objects.

For Libeskind, it was the impossible questions that mattered most: How to give voice to an absent Jewish culture without presuming to speak for it? How to bridge an open wound without mending it? How to house under a single roof a panoply of diametric oppositions and contradictions? He thus allowed his drawings to work through the essential paradoxes at the heart of his project: How to give form to a void without filling it in? How to give architectural form to the formless and to challenge the very attempt to house such memory?

Before beginning to work, Libeskind supplanted the very name used to describe the Senate's project, "Extension of the Berlin Museum with the Jewish Museum Department," with his own more poetic title, "Between the Lines." "I call it ["Between the Lines"] because it is a project about two lines of thinking, organization, and relationship," Libeskind wrote. "One is a straight line, but broken into many fragments; the other is a tortuous line, but continuing indefinitely. These two lines develop architecturally and programmatically through a limited but definite dialogue.

They also fall apart, become disengaged, and are seen as separated. In this way, they expose a void that runs through this museum and through architecture, a discontinuous void."[14] Through a contorted and zigzagging lightning bolt of a building, Libeskind drove a void and unusable space that literally sliced through and beyond it. According to Libeskind, the extension was conceived "as an emblem where the not visible has made itself apparent as a void, an invisible. . . . The idea is very simple: to build the museum around a void that runs through it, a void that is to be experienced by the public."[15] As he makes clear, this void is indeed the building's structural rib, its main axis, a central bearing wall that bears only its own absence.

Indeed, as became clear in the first walk-through of the still-empty building in the late 1990s, it was not the building itself that constituted Libeskind's architecture, but the spaces inside the building, the voids and absence embodied by empty spaces: that which was constituted not by the lines of his drawings, but by spaces between the lines. By building voids into the heart of his design, Libeskind thus highlighted the spaces between walls as the primary element of his architecture. The walls were important only insofar as they lent shape to these spaces and defined their borders. But ultimately, it was the void "between the lines" that Libeskind sought to capture here, a void so real, so palpable, and so elemental to Jewish history in Berlin as to be its focal point after the Holocaust – a negative center of gravity around which Jewish memory would now assemble.[16]

Implied in any museum's collection is that what you see is all there is to see, all that there ever was. By inserting architectural "voids" into the museum,

Libeskind has reversed the terms of this museological assumption. What you see here, he seems to say, is actually only a mask for all that is missing, for the great absence of life that now makes a presentation of these artifacts a necessity. The voids make palpable the sense that much more is missing here than can ever be shown. As Vera Bendt aptly noted, it was destruction itself that caused the collection in this museum to come into being. Otherwise, these objects would all belong to living, breathing families; they would be installed in private homes, not the exhibition spaces of a museum. This is then an aggressively anti-redemptory design, literally built around an absence of meaning in history, the absence of the people whose lives gave meaning to these objects, and to their history.

But with its 30 connecting bridges, its 7,000 square meters of permanent exhibition space, 450 square meters of temporary exhibition space, and 4,000 square meters of storage, office, and auditorium spaces, the Jewish Museum Berlin occupies roughly three times the space of the Berlin Museum. Some have suggested that the Berlin Museum be allowed to spill into most of the newly available space, leaving the Jewish Museum Berlin the bottom floor only; others have suggested that the building in its entirety be designated the national "memorial to Europe's murdered Jews."[17] In any case, the attention this design has received since the museum was inaugurated in September 2001 has begun to generate a final historical irony. Where the city planners had hoped to return Jewish memory to the house of Berlin's own history, it now seems certain that Berlin's history faces the task of finding its place in the larger haunted house of Jewish memory. The Jewish extension to the Berlin Museum has become the prism through which the rest of the world will come to know Berlin's own past.

Even though the Jewish Museum Berlin was Daniel Libeskind's first museum commission, it was not the first of his museums to be built. That was the Felix-Nussbaum-Museum in Osnabrück, Germany, proposed in 1995 and completed in 1998. Again this began with a proposal for an extension to an existing museum, this time the Kulturgeschichtliches Museum, or Cultural History Museum, of Osnabrück. Sharing the site with the 1888–89 building housing the Cultural History Museum was the Villa Schlikker of 1900–01, which was appropriated as headquarters of the Nazy Party from 1933 to 1945, today a museum of everyday life and culture, the House of Remembering. Libeskind's approach was to find a way to reconnect the town back to itself, to its history, its loss, the murder of one of its native Jewish sons, an artist, as emblematic of the larger mass murder perpetrated in Germany's name.

The recovery in the early 1970s of a trove of paintings by Felix Nussbaum, works produced in Berlin before World War II, prompted the small German industrial city of Osnabrück, his birthplace, to begin the process of establishing a permanent home for them. Nussbaum himself was barely known to the public until 1985, when New York's Jewish Museum presented a retrospective exhibition that traveled widely in Europe and Israel. Born in 1904 to a Jewish family in Osnabrück, Nussbaum enjoyed great success as a young artist, studying painting in Hamburg and Berlin before moving to Rome in 1932 when he was awarded the coveted two-year Villa Massimo Scholarship by the German Academy. By this time, Nussbaum had produced a remarkable body of portraits of himself

and his family, landscapes, and city views, many of which were lost to a fire in his Berlin atelier in 1932 while he was living abroad.

With the rise to power of Hitler and the Nazi Party in 1933, Nussbaum never set foot in Germany again. He was forced to move from Rome to Monte Carlo, then to Paris. In 1934, he and the love of his life, Felka Platek, the painter with whom he set off for Rome, were granted tourist visas to Belgium for the following year. They settled first in Ostend, then married in 1937 and moved to Brussels. He continued to paint, but his horizons narrowed with the outbreak of war in 1939. With the German invasion of Belgium in 1940, Nussbaum was arrested and imprisoned at the internment camp at Saint-Cyprien in the south of France. He escaped and made his way back to Brussels, but had to go into hiding to avoid discovery. His paintings of 1935 began to mirror his increasingly desperate and ever-more constrained circumstances. By the time of his second arrest by the Nazis and his eventual deportation to Auschwitz in 1944, Nussbaum had amassed an unparalleled corpus of work, which today is considered emblematic of the plight of European Jews during World War II.

"How does one express architecturally the aspirations, the realities, the despair of a Jewish painter from Osnabrück in those years ending in tragedy?" Libeskind asked in his 1995 project description for the museum. How to represent such a life in architecture? In a 1995 lecture entitled "Museum without Exit," Libeskind answered by describing his design which comprises three volumes, the German oak-clad Nussbaum Haus, the concrete Nussbaum Corridor, and the zinc-clad Nussbaum Bridge:

The first is a very traditional wooden building which stands on the site in a special relationship to the old synagogue on Rolandstrasse, which was burned in 1938 [during Kristallnacht]. I made a kind of traditional wooden building for about 300 works painted in the 1920s and early 1930s. That wooden space is violently cut by a dramatic volume standing 11 meters high, 50 meters long: the Nussbaum Gang or corridor. It is only two meters in width, the narrowest volume that can be built as a public space under German regulations. It is made of concrete, has no windows of any sort. And there I proposed to show the works of Nussbaum created during his race through Europe. Whilst a fugitive, he lived in tiny rooms and painted in very close quarters. He could not stand back from the works to look at them. He painted in secret in a kind of delirium. . . . These paintings and drawings, sometimes created by [him] inches away, have only been viewed close up, never from some aesthetic distancing.[18]

There is a stark contrast between the Nussbaum Haus installation of paintings dating from before 1932, and Libeskind's concept for the Nussbaum Corridor, where he reproduced the claustrophobic quarters of the artist's own work space and the diminishing horizons experienced in his flight from the Nazis. This stark volume has the effect of forcing visitors to experience these paintings and the life they represent from an uncomfortably close, personal range. The Nussbaum Corridor funnels visitors into the museum's third volume, what Libeskind calls the Nussbaum Brücke or bridge, a long, zinc-clad building suspended above ground and connected to the adjacent Cultural History

Museum. In descriptions of the project, Libeskind wrote that:

> This "bridge-building" houses the recently discovered paintings of Nussbaum, works from which even the signature of Nussbaum had been erased. The gallery spaces are on two levels opening from the corridor. The Nussbaum Brücke brings the past into the future, spanning the gaps and hollows traced by the two other building volumes. It physically connects Nussbaum to the Cultural History Museum. The Felix-Nussbaum-Haus incorporates not only the spirit of the artist, but also the physical and kinetic enclosure of the fragmented, broken, cut, light-dark world of Felix Nussbaum, the Jew, the painter, the Osnabrücker, the citizen of Germany and Europe.

The sequence of materials similarly reflects the stages of the artist's life: the native German oak of Nussbaum Haus, the blank of the concrete Nussbaum Corridor, the cold metal cladding of the Nussbaum Brücke together represent the journey from Nussbaum's birthplace to a cold and indifferent exile, and back again. Where the installation abruptly ends on the second floor of the Nussbaum Bridge, Libeskind invokes the artist's thwarted path to safety and refuge, literally a life-path cut short. The rupture occurs where Felix-Nusbaum-Haus connects to the Cultural History Museum, in which Osnabrück's history is narrated and documented. Thus does Libeskind's building attempt to reincorporate the town's native son and artist into the town's history and memory, but also to represent by its spatial disjunctures the impossibility of completing that gesture – not unlike Libeskind's strategy for the Jewish Museum Berlin.

At its heart, this complex has no structural center of gravity, but is rather a loose aggregate of old and new buildings, linked but also separate. The complex is not legible from any single vantage point, being an ensemble of disparate parts that cohere only in the visitor's memory. This coherence is predicated on the power of the three volumes of Felix-Nussbaum-Haus to prevent the whole from falling apart. Libeskind sought to connect the two existing and three new buildings and to simultaneously evoke the lost life of an exiled son returned to his birthplace, a nation burdened with the indelible memory of its crimes – but always in a way that attempts and thwarts or renders impossible full reconciliation.

Here in fact, Libeskind's architecture, like Nussbaum's paintings, expresses a resistance to classical notions of harmony and balance. The aggressively acute, almost jagged angles serve as reminders of senseless destruction and echo the artist's own increasingly anguished soul. Both the paintings and the spaces that contain them remain radically out of balance and jarring in their disharmonies. In such architecture, there is no pretense to the restoration of a ruptured civilization, by which the signs of death and destruction are rendered invisible. In the Japanese tradition of urushi, broken crockery is repaired by using gold inlay to make visible, even to highlight, the damage, which shows that a household object has lived, weathered life, survived, and wears its scars with dignity. In the artist Barbara Bloom's wise meditation on urushi, she describes how she was "struck by the beauty of an accepted and accentuated imperfection with no attempt to cover up or disappear history."[19] As an aesthetic strategy, privileging the visibility of a repair rather than repressing it seems to be a gesture that embraces life in all of its dislocations and breaches and offers the redemption of destruction through beauty. Our post-Holocaust eyes see only the irreparability of the Holocaust, the irredeemable destruction of Europe's Jews, the forever shattered past. Any attempted repair must make itself felt as pain and breach. It is a subtle difference, but one Libeskind has navigated very deliberately: how to reveal the break without appearing to mend it, how to give form to brokenness without beautifying it, how to articulate loss without filling it in.

Throughout Europe, where vibrant Jewish communities have lived for centuries, there are only museums to their destruction. And although museums dedicated to the memory of the Jewish past have come into being to tell the stories of those communities, in countries where few Jews survived, they may also constitute the only remaining Jewish presence. Theodor Adorno's melancholy observation that "the German word *museal* . . . describes objects to which the observer no longer has a vital relationship and which are in the process of dying" seems all too apt a description of Jewish museums in Europe.[20] Premised as they are on the violent extirpation of Jewish life on European soil which reduced a 1,000-year-old civilization to a few scattered artifacts, these museums indeed view the Jewish past through its broken vessels.

The exception that seems to prove this rule, of course, is Denmark, whose mobilization to rescue its Jewish citizens from Nazi capture and deportation still serves as a beacon for what "might have been done" anywhere else. Tipped off in the last days of September 1943 that the Nazi SS were about to begin a round-up of Denmark's 8,000 Jews, local

Danish and Jewish resistance organizers under the umbrella of the Danish Freedom Council evacuated all but 485 Danish Jews from their homes. By the time the Germans began their sweep on the night of October 2, 1943, most of Denmark's Jews had been secretly shuttled to the coast, where Danish fishing boats ferried them, making some 700 voyages back and forth, to Sweden, where they were given refuge. Denmark's 400-year-old Jewish community, longintegrated into Danish society, was thus preserved in one of the most stunning humanitarian operations of World War II.[21]

Though the rescue of Danish Jewry occupies a singular place in Holocaust and European Jewish history, it was never intended by the founders of the Danish Jewish Museum to be a locus for housing the culture, art, and history of Denmark's Jewish community. In fact, the idea of a Jewish museum in Denmark had been bruited about for nearly a century, and several exhibitions of art and artifacts from the Royal Library's mammoth and well-preserved collections of Judaica were mounted between 1908 and 1984, when the present museum was first proposed by the Society for Danish Jewish History. Several possible locations for the Danish Jewish Museum were discussed. One of the founding board members suggested the soaring vaulted spaces of the 16th-century Royal Boat House in Copenhagen, originally built to store the Royal Navy's fleet, but mainly used as a storehouse for cannons until 1902 when its upper floors were removed and the vaulted ground floor was incorporated into the Royal Library. The Danish Ministry of Culture and the Royal Library agreed, and granted tenancy to the newly constituted Danish Jewish Museum, allowing it to occupy two of the building's five vaulted bays.

It was with this maritime history in mind that Daniel Libeskind accepted the commission of the Danish Jewish Museum in the early 1990s. Several of Denmark's schools of architecture as well as the Royal Danish Academy of Fine Arts had already invited Libeskind as a visiting professor. Thus he was already known and admired by the museum's founding board when they invited him to design the new Danish Jewish Museum. It was also clear to him that the site was perfect in both its location and its maritime references, which for him resonated most poignantly with the boat rescue of Denmark's Jews during World War II. As Libeskind has explained in his text describing the design process, because this extraordinarily great deed distinguishes Denmark's past and present from other European Jewish histories, the "organizing principle" of Danish Jewish Museum is the concept of *mitzvah* — the Hebrew word meaning "a fundamental good deed." While most of what "happens" in Libeskind's design takes place inside the exhibition halls, which are "both written and read like a text within a text within a text," invoking the structure of the Talmud, whose central text is surrounded by layer upon layer of intertextual commentary, he also talks about its "urban and architectural aspects," how it ties the adjacent Black Diamond, the new library building completed in 1999 to the old Royal Library building by activating the pedestrian walk along the former Victualing Yard or Proviantgården in the interior courtyard of the Royal Library, where, for Libeskind, "water and a symbolic rowboat dramatically speak to the uniqueness of the survival of the Danish Jewish community."

In stark contrast to the broken paths, interrupted narratives, and dead ends that characterize

Libeskind's Jewish museums in Berlin and Osnabrück, Libeskind strove to make the organization of artifacts and the visitor's path "seamless," invoking the fundamental integration of the Danish Jewish community into its larger cultural and urban surroundings. However, despite its "seamless" narrative structure, Libeskind's Danish Jewish Museum nevertheless surprises visitors as they traverse its highly idiosyncratic matrix of four slightly sloping floor planes (not unlike standing on a ship moving through rolling waves), which are bathed in angled deltas of light – all penetrated by a unifying "virtual plane" that becomes actual surface for exhibition purposes. Libeskind has noted that this is a "visual vector that extends the visitor's experience beyond the walls of the museum": the entire sensory and spatial experience of the museum is conceived as seamless and surprising, a fitting counterpart to the history of Denmark's Jews. This is an architecture of discovery, framed and thus informed by the history of a seafaring people, and by the memory of an astonishing sea rescue that resulted, over all these many years, in an unbroken chain of Jewish life, culture, and art in a small Scandinavian country where Jews have long been at home.

Libeskind's Contemporary Jewish Museum marks yet another shift in the paradigm of Jewish museum. From the time of its founding, it has hosted dozens of original and traveling exhibitions of Jewish art and culture as well as other types of events and programming. Without a permanent collection of art or artifacts to weigh it down, it was always "of-the-moment" – even when its shows examined the Jewish past. For a brief period in the early 1990s, the Jewish Museum San Francisco merged with the Judah Magnes Museum in Berkeley,

with its extensive collection of Judaica from California and the American West. The two institutions eventually demerged, and the Contemporary Jewish Museum (CJM) emerged, affirming in its new name the mission of a museum dedicated to the Jewish present. Without a permanent collection to house, to cultivate, or to influence the nature of its programming, the CJM regained its identity as an institution ever-responsive to its place in the cultural dialogue between Jewish and non-Jewish worlds. In its celebration of this contemporary give-and-take, it would eventually affirm its core identity as a space for contemporary Jewish life.

In 1995, the city of San Francisco awarded the museum one of its prized landmark buildings, the 1881 Jessie Street Power Substation renovated in 1906 by Willis Polk. Proposing this site in the heart of the Yerba Buena redevelopment district, in the vicinity of the soon-to-be-completed Museum of Modern Art and the evolving Moscone Convention Center, in a district that was fast attracting other cultural institutions, city planners could not possibly have known at the time that they would receive such a gem of a building in return. Guided by clear-eyed recommendations for the preservation of a highly admired building in the tradition of the City Beautiful Movement, which aimed "to transform utilitarian structures into handsome civic ornaments," the museum's building committee decided right at the start that this was going to be something new from something old.

In fact, the museum was awarded the landmark building at least partly because planners recognized that its central mission was to preserve the past and assimilate it to the present, thereby bringing it back to life. In the words of one of its earliest drafts, the museum's Architectural Building Program suggested that "the idea of 'dialogue' plays an important role in Jewish culture; it is the mode of narration of the Bible – the dialectic between man and God. . . . Spaces which evoke dynamic tension, which contain interplaying forms, which convey the distance and connection of the earthly and spiritual – all these might reflect the 'dialectic'. The interrelation of creator and creation/artist and art is another manifestation."[22] With the preservation philosophies of both the museum and the city in such accord, it seemed like a perfect match. Three years later, in 1998, Daniel Libeskind was awarded his first American building commission.

The Jessie Street Power Substation was not preserved in its entirety, but the shell and a number of other features were restored or adapted, in particular, the aspect that architectural historians like Paul Turner have regarded as the most brilliant feature of the building: its great south-facing facade, the wall. As Turner made clear in his 1974 report on the architectural significance of the building, the original commission's call "for a large simple mass and unencumbered wall-surfaces gave Polk the perfect opportunity to concentrate on an eminently Classical problem: the design of a wall, as an abstract and highly sophisticated composition of architectural elements."[23] With its "large arch, the seven elegantly detailed windows at the right, the smaller doorway with its consoled entablature supporting a sculptural grouping of putti with garlands, the cornices and dentil-courses at the top of the facade, and the expanses of the plain brick wall itself," Turner concluded that Polk's "could be thought of as an excellent case-study of the monumental possibilities

in the design of a mere wall." The building was deemed worthy of preservation not owing to its function as a power station, but because it embodied so exquisitely the City Beautiful credo of that era. Polk's south facade had come to represent an architectural moment of awakening, a civic impulse to turn all buildings – no matter how utilitarian – into beautiful objects.

Quoting a Getty Conservation Institute (GCI) report published at about the same time that the Jessie Street Power Substation was granted to the museum, the building committee expressed their thinking about preservation issues: "We would not have the monument of old but a monument that emerges anew – an independent architectural expression, even if fragmentary, that respects the basic integrity of what the past has handed down to us."[24] According to the structure report on Polk's facade, as difficult as it may be to integrate a monumental relic into a new building, the possible rewards are great. Here again the museum cited the GCI report to make their case:

> It is a matter of giving back to the object or to the architectural element to be restored not only a worthy physical context, but a figurative context – no longer the original one that is lost or irrecoverable, nor the atrophied and incomprehensible one of a too-badly damaged image. The new context has to derive from placing the object in a new 'artistic work', so the object becomes part of the structure into which it is inserted, by maintaining an independent legibility and by joining with other new elements. . . . It would be a redesigned image with the existing remains used and reinserted next to new elements, creating a figurative 'circuit'. We would not have the

monument of old but a monument that emerges anew — an independent architectural expression even if fragmentary, that respects the basic integrity of what the past has handed down to us.[25]

As becomes clear when standing in the plaza facing the wall, both the museum's building committee and the architect took these ideas to heart. The wall maintains both an "independent legibility" and "emerges anew" — even as it serves formally as both screen and gateway for Libeskind's new building.

I wondered if this wall was what attracted Libeskind to the site in the first place. He admitted that it was part of the attraction, especially as an abstract form that could both join and divide, hide and reveal. And what about its origin as an exemplar of the City Beautiful Movement, I asked? What would it mean to preserve it as a remnant of another time altogether? This, too, he thought was intriguing. In Jewish tradition, after all, attention is paid to remnant walls (think of the Western Wall in Jerusalem). Indeed, it was while Libeskind was designing the CJM in its relation to Polk's south facade that he was suddenly pulled into a new project as Master Designer of the new World Trade Center complex after 9/11. One of the most powerful elements of his winning design for the Freedom Tower and Memory Foundations was his commitment to preserve and prominently feature the slurry walls of the World Trade Center site, to remember how they held back the harbor waters despite the mammoth collapse of the towers. Derisively called a "wailing wall" by Rafael Viñoly during the presentation of his and Libeskind's site plan proposals for Lower Manhattan, the focus on the wall and all its traditional, literal, and figurative echoes made

perfect sense to Libeskind at the time. Whether consciously or not, the architect's preoccupation with the idea of the wall has informed both projects — as different as they are.

In his review of Libeskind's early scheme for the Contemporary Jewish Museum, Nicolai Ouroussoff wrote, "Rather than try to smooth over the forces that shape a modern metropolis, [Libeskind's building] seeks to express them in architectural form."[26] That is, even the messiness of urban renewal is given formal recognition here. In words that echo the very mission of the CJM, Libeskind has commented that "no one can survive isolated from the culture that surrounds them." Moreover, by proposing a design that tucks his building behind the existing facade, into a small space, making no attempt to dominate surrounding buildings, Libeskind has taken what could have been just another constraint, the lack of space in a dense urban site, and made of it a benevolent gesture to the building's neighbors. In this vein, Ouroussoff also pointed out that the decision to preserve the Jessie Street Power Substation's original shell and facade loads the museum with multiple meanings, a parable for aspects of the modern Jewish condition: "The desire to conform to existing conditions and rebel against them can be read as a metaphor for the Jewish struggle with issues of identity and assimilation."[27]

The result may be Daniel Libeskind's most self-effacing, but most "neighborly" building yet. Make no mistake, it is audacious in its angled and animated exterior planes, very much its own jewel in the urban firmament. But it is also understated, content in its relatively small scale, dwarfed by the Four Seasons Hotel abutting its north side, and partially hidden by the historic red-brick walls out of which it peeks, almost as if the earth buckled and pushed up a polished and faceted blue-steel gemstone. As a diamond is produced by the supercompression of gigantic earth forces, this gem of a building emerges from what the architect calls "the energy of a complex urban center."

Because of its location, tucked tightly behind the brick of the former power substation and wedged against the Four Seasons Hotel next to a pedestrian passageway and across from what will be the Mexican Museum, the CJM is not wholly visible from anywhere, but seen from everywhere in context with its neighbors. As a model for Jewish integration, the building and its location speak volumes. In other words, it is not part of the San Francisco skyline, but more a treasure tucked into a pocket of Yerba Buena's museum district. Conversely, its interior sight lines take in nearly every gallery, window, and wall of the museum. It is, in other words, a self-effacing building that brings its surroundings inside, rather than projecting itself front and center onto the city's architectural stage.

Referring to its tight quarters, the architect remarked that "there's almost no space for this building," and he's right.[28] The building's space is all on the inside, looking out at its urban surroundings: St. Patrick's Catholic Church, the Martin Luther King Memorial, the pedestrian walkway, the future Mexican Museum, and the Yerba Buena Gardens across the street. The historic facade functions as a portal into the museum's inner space, where life, culture, and memory are lived. When viewed from the plaza on the site's south side, the wall functions as both scrim and portal, creating the illusion of a relatively

modest exterior housing an enormous set of interior galleries.

At first glance, the Second Floor Gallery seems to echo the jagged lines and angles of the Jewish Museum Berlin. But as Ouroussoff pointed out, "Internal terraces are cut out of the upper portion, allowing you to see into the entry hall and visually linking past and present." That is, these jagged cuts and angles create and open up volumes, unlike the slashing voids designed to interrupt and cut off any open, narrative flow in the Jewish Museum Berlin, as constant reminders of the historical breach of the Holocaust.

In stark contrast to the interrupted and occluded sight lines of the Jewish museums in Berlin and Osnabrück, almost every place in the interior of the CJM is visible from any other place. All can be seen at once as an integrated and transparent whole, with unobstructed sight lines. Unlike the explicitly Holocaust-inflected museums of Berlin, Osnabrück, and to a lesser extent, Copenhagen – which are cut through with sharp angles, architectural gestures that invoke violent deeds – San Francisco's Contemporary Jewish Museum is designed as an unbroken or "whole space." Whereas the signature features of his previous Jewish museums involve what one critic called the "absence of rectilinear space, the anonymous box replaced by colliding forms, tilted floors, and canted walls," the most significant element of the CJM may be the fluid openness created by still-angled but now voluminous gallery spaces that all connect and flow into one another.[29]

As such, it becomes a spatial metaphor for the integration of Jewish and non-Jewish cultures and the free exchange between old and new. In its outward-looking spaces, the CJM reminds us that Jewish culture is always produced in dialogue with surrounding cultures, just as surrounding cultures have always been constituted in their exchanges with Jewish culture. In this view, Jewish culture is constituted in the reciprocal exchange with other cultures, rather than a hermetically sealed monologue with itself. By letting in the light of its surroundings, the CJM is vivified and sustained by exchange with the community as much as its architectural neighbors.

In his review of the Contemporary Jewish Museum, Gabriel Sanders of *Forward* aptly cited a groundbreaking sociological study by Steven M. Cohen and Ari Kelman describing the current mind-set of young, largely unaffiliated Jews. "From our interviews with Jewish young adults," Cohen and Kelman reported, "we learned how 'engaged, but unaffiliated' Jews seek cultural experiences that offer alternatives to an institutional world they see as bland, conformist, conservative and alien. Instead, they are drawn to events that promise to cross boundaries between Jews and non-Jews, Jews and Jews, Jewish space and non-Jewish space, and distinctively Jewish culture with putatively non-Jewish culture, effecting a 'cultural hybridity'."[30] In this extraordinary statement, they captured the goal of the museum, which is to offer space where Jewish and non-Jewish cultures coexist, reciprocally nourish, and inspire one another. Rather than definitively resolving the issue of what constitutes Jewish art, the CJM becomes a space where both Jewish and non-Jewish visitors ponder the question. In its first show, organized around the book of Genesis, Jewish and non-Jewish artists were invited to explore their

relations to what might be regarded as the Jewish Ur-text, Genesis.

With the mandate to design a museum focused on Jewish life and culture in the present, rather than the past, Libeskind has incorporated into the design two Hebrew letters, *chet* and *yud*, which make up the word for life, *chai* – expressing through these abstractions the spirit of life lived in the present moment, inflected (but not oppressed) by memory of the past. The life of this building does not depend on the symbolic significance of the Hebrew letters; rather they animate the spaces which are themselves designed for life. "In the Jewish tradition," Libeskind reminds us, "letters are not mere signs, but are substantial participants in the story they create."[31]

In this case, of course, it is their literal spatiality that bestows meaning on the kind of story being told. As Libeskind explained in his description of the project, "the Chet provides an overall continuity for the exhibition and educational spaces, and the Yud ... gives a new identity to the power substation." The *yud* is, of course, the flying first letter of the sacred tetragrammaton יהוה (YHVH) – the unutterable name of G-d – and the last letter in the Hebrew word for life, *chai* (*chet-yud*). According to philosopher Elliot R. Wolfson, "The image of the *yud* in the brain to symbolize the attribute of wisdom set in the middle and encompassing everything is found in the commentary of Sefer Yesirah that preserves the teachings of Isaac the Blind."[32] In the context of Libeskind's new building, the Yud actually lodges its wondrously voluminous and tranquil space within the minds of those inside it. It is as if the smallest letter of the alphabet has been miraculously inflated, expanded into the largest single space in the museum, an open space inviting near-mystical contemplation and wonder.

Just as sometimes a poem is not all about meaning, but about sound and sense, space and the inward search for meaning, Libeskind's architecture is not just about housing life or culture, or even about making life and culture meaningful. It is also about making space in which we find ourselves unexpectedly transported, without ever leaving; it reveals juxtapositions of time and space, and generates visual dialogues that we have never before seen or imagined.

Daniel Libeskind's Jewish museum designs, to my mind, signal a return to the conceptual religious foundations of Jewish architecture. With his formal emphasis on the spaces "between the lines," on the opening of internal volumes where communities gather to explore cultural expression, the architect reinforces Judaism's starting point for sacred space, the quorum or *Minyan* of ten Jews gathered to pray, rather than a building in and of itself.[33] Likewise, as Carol Herselle Krinsky reminds us, "the very word *synagogue* comes from the Greek *synagein*, to bring together."[34] That is, just as a prayer *Minyan* turns any space into Jewish sacred space, akin to the Temple of Jerusalem, "Jewish architecture" is rooted in conceptual space, constituted not by formal structural elements, walls and cornices, but by what goes on within the volume of that space. Moreover, even the Temple of Jerusalem is figured in the Bible both as a physical place and more abstractly as a space carried within oneself, as Krinsky notes:

When the captives mourned their loss of the Temple [in Jerusalem], the prophet Ezekiel consoled them with the words that the Lord had spoken to him: "Thus says the Lord God: Although I removed them far off among the nations, and although I have scattered them among the countries, yet have I been as a little sanctuary in the countries where they are come."[35]

Though Jews may build sacrificial shrines to imitate the lost one in Jerusalem, according to Krinsky, "spiritual sanctuary" was always more an abstract figure than a literal building, carried in the hearts and minds of the faithful. In this view, God's sanctuary is carried within Jews who keep faith, embodied by the assembly of prayer – not by the house in which they profess such faith.

In this light, Jewish architecture is less about the building's space in the landscape and more about the space such buildings open up inside us for prayer and contemplation, for our individual contemplation of the Jewish relationship to God, life, history, culture, and identity. Jewish architecture consists of this exchange between Jews and the buildings they inhabit, not in a particular building design. As such, Jewish architecture remains unfixed, underdetermined, contingent on new times, inhabitants, meanings, and uses. In the absence of the vitality and memory of Jewish lives that have inhabited it, however, Jewish architecture can also revert to the status of monument only – ossified in time and space, without Jewish meaning.

ENDNOTES

1 Anthony Lane, "The Shutterbug," *The New Yorker*, May 21, 2001: 80.
2 Max Kozloff, *New York: Capital of Photography*, exh. cat. (New Haven and London: Yale University Press and New York: The Jewish Museum, 2002), p. 70.
3 Bruno Zevi, *Ebraismo e Architettura* (Florence: Editrice La Giuntina, 1993), p. 83. As quoted in English and German translations by Thorsten Rodiek, *Daniel Libeskind – Museum ohne Ausgang: Das Felix-Nussbaum-Haus des Kulturgeschichtlichen Museums Osnabrück* (Tübingen and Berlin: Ernst Wasmuth Verlag, 1998), pp. 68, 111, n. 77.
4 Gavriel Rosenfeld, "Ground Zero as a Lab for New Art," *Forward*, February 21, 2003.
5 See Nathaniel Popper, "Transforming Tragedies into Memorable Memorials" [interview with the author], *Forward*, January 16, 2004.
6 See Maya Lin, *Boundaries* (New York: Simon & Schuster, 2000), 4:09. Lin's reference to the Pingusson memorial in Paris was made in conversation with the author.
7 See Vera Bendt, "Das Jüdische Museum," in *Wegweiser durch das jüdische Berlin: Geschichte und Gegenwart* (Berlin: Nicolai Verlag, 1987), pp. 200–209.
8 Quoted in Martina Weinland and Kurt Winkler, *Das Jüdische Museum im Stadtmuseum Berlin: Eine Dokumentation/The Jewish Museum in the Berlin Municipal Museum: A Record* (Berlin: Nicolai, 1997), p. 10.
9 The issue of what constitutes Jewish art remains as fraught as ever in contemporary discussions of national and ethnic art. Among other discussions of the subject, see Joseph Gutmann, "Is There a Jewish Art?" in *The Visual Dimension: Aspects of Jewish Art*, ed. Claire Moore (Boulder, Co.: Westview Press, 1993), pp. 1–20.
10 Weinland and Winkler, *Das Jüdische Museum im Stadtmuseum Berlin*, p. 10.
11 See Rolf Bothe and Vera Bendt, "Ein eigenstandiges Judisches Museum als Abteilung des Berlin Museums," in *Realisierungswettbewerb: Erweiterung Berlin Museum mit Abteilung Jüdisches Museum* (Berlin: Senatsverwaltung fur Bau- und Wohnungswesen, 1990), p. 12.
12 "Nichts in Berlins Geschichte hat die Stadt jemals mehr verandert als die Verfolgung, Verteibung und Ermordung ihrer judischen Burger – dies war eine Veranderung nach Innen, die ins Herz der Stadt traf," from *Realisierungswettbewerb*, p. 12; the emphasis is my own.
13 Bothe and Bendt, *Realisierungswettbewerb*, p. 169.
14 Daniel Libeskind, *Between the Lines: Extension to the Berlin Museum with the Jewish Museum* (Amsterdam: Joods Historisch Museum, 1991), p. 3.
15 Daniel Libeskind, "Between the Lines," in *Daniel Libeskind: Erweiterung des Berlin Museums mit Abteilung Jüdisches Museum*, ed. Kristin Feireiss (Berlin: Ernst & Sohn, 1992), p. 63.
16 For further insightful reflection on role these voids play in Berlin generally and in Libeskind's design, in particular, see Andreas Huyssen, "The Voids of Berlin," *Critical Inquiry* 24:1 (Fall 1997): 57–81.
17 See James E. Young, *At Memory's Edge: After-Images of the Holocaust in Contemporary Art and Architecture* (New Haven and London: Yale University Press, 2000), on which the present essay is based, and in which I give the entire account of Germany's national "Memorial for the Murdered Jews of Europe" in Berlin, including Libeskind's proposed design. In submitting a design for this memorial, the architect made clear that he did not want his museum design for a Jewish museum to be turned into a Holocaust memorial.
18 Daniel Libeskind, "Project Description," Studio Daniel Libeskind, 1995.
19 Barbara Bloom, "Broken," *The Collections of Barbara Bloom*, exh. cat. (New York: International Center of Photography and Steidl, 2007), p. 190.
20 Theodor W. Adorno, "Valery Proust Museum," in *Prisms*, trans. Samuel Weber and Shierry Weber Nicholson (Cambridge, Mass.: The MIT Press, 1981), p. 175.
21 Among other accounts, see *The Rescue of the Danish Jews: Moral Courage under Stress*, ed. Leo Goldberger (New York: New York University Press, 1987), pp. 3–12.
22 "Preservation Philosophy," in the Jewish Museum of San Francisco's Draft Architectural Building Program of June 1996, p. 46.
23 Paul V. Turner, "Report on the Architectural Significance of Existing Structures in the Yerba Buena Center Area, San Francisco," September 10, 1974 (unpublished manuscript).
24 Giovanni Carbonara, "The Integration of the Image: Problems in the Restoration of Monuments," excerpted in *Historical and Philosophical Issues in the Conservation of Cultural Heritage*, Nicholas Stanley Price, M. Kirby Talley, Jr., and Alessandra Melucco Vaccaro, eds. (Los Angeles: Getty Trust Publications and Getty Conservation Institute 1996) p. 238.
25 Carbonara, "The Integration of the Image," pp. 239–40.
26 Nicolai Ouroussoff, "Conflict and Harmony Together in One Design," *Los Angeles Times*, April 2, 2000, p. 65.
27 Ouroussoff, "Conflict and Harmony Together in One Design," p. 65.
28 See Alec Appelbaum, "Plans for the Future," *Nextbook.org*, January 29, 2008.
29 Victoria Newhouse, "Designs that Reach Out and Grab," *The New York Times*, June 4, 2000, Arts and Leisure section, p. 36.
30 Gabriel Sanders, "They're Building It, but Will They Come?" *Forward*, November 23, 2007, section B, p. 4.
31 Appelbaum, "Plans for the Future."
32 Elliot R. Wolfson, *Language, Eros, and Being: Kabbalistic Hermeneutics and Poetic Imagination* (New York: Fordham University Press, 2006), p. 453, n. 197.
33 Sanhedrin, 2B.
34 Carol Herselle Krinsky, *Synagogues of Europe: Architecture, History, Meaning* (Cambridge, Mass. and London: The MIT Press, 1985), p. 5.
35 Krinsky, *Synagogues of Europe*, p. 5 (Ezekiel, 11.16).

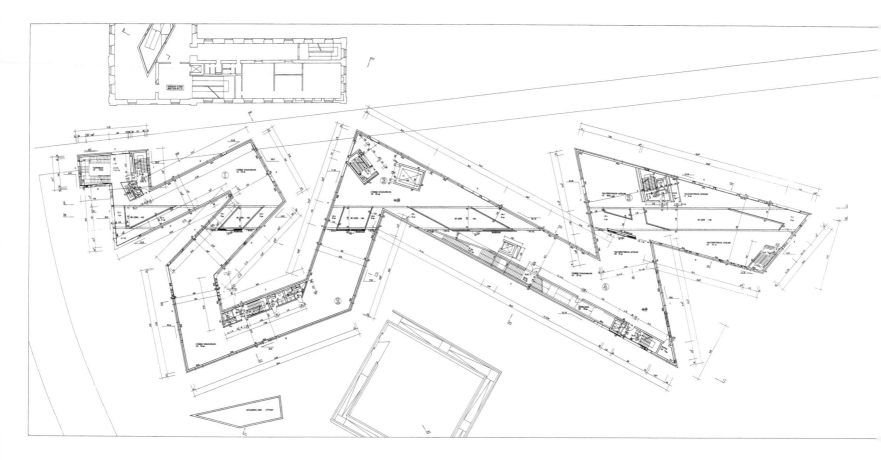

When I was invited by the Berlin Senate to participate in the 1988 competition for an extension to accommodate a Jewish department of the Stadtmuseum Berlin, I felt that this was not a program I had to invent, but one in which I was implicated from the beginning, having been born only a few hundred kilometers east of Berlin in Lodz, Poland, and having lost most of my family in the Holocaust. "Between the Lines" is the name I gave the project, because it is about two lines of thinking, organization, and relationship. One is a straight line, broken into many fragments, the other a tortuous line, continuing indefinitely.

The site was in the old center of Berlin, which has once again become the center. The Stadtmuseum was housed in the Baroque Kollegienhaus on Lindenstrasse (1734-35), commissioned by Friedrich Wilhelm I as the first Prussian Court of Justice and renovated in the 1960s as a museum for the city of Berlin. In approaching the site, although it was an actual, physical place, I understood it as an invisible matrix of connections, of entwined relationships between the figures of Germans and the figures of Jews. This idea led to the fourfold structure of the project, and which ultimately led to a transformation of the existing museum: the entire complex is known today as the Jewish Museum Berlin.

Considering that the competition was staged a year before the Berlin Wall came down, I felt there was a feature common to both East and West Berlin which bound them together: the relationship of Germans to Jews. Workers, writers, composers, artists, scientists, and poets have forged a link between Jewish tradition and German culture. I used this connection to plot an irrational matrix that yielded references to the emblematic image of a compressed and distorted star - the yellow star that was so frequently worn on this very site. The zigzagging form of the distorted star was the first aspect of the project.

I have always been interested in the music of Arnold Schönberg and, in particular, his Berlin period. In Schönberg's greatest work, the opera *Moses and Aaron*, the logic of the libretto could not be completed by the musical score. At the end, Moses doesn't sing, he merely speaks "Oh Word, thou Word," addressing the absence of the Word. We understand it as a text, because when the singing stops, Moses utters the missing Word, the call for the Word, the call for the Deed. With the project for a Jewish museum in Berlin, I sought to complete Schönberg's opera architecturally. That was is the second aspect of the project.

The third aspect was my interest in the names of those who were deported from Berlin during the fatal years of the Holocaust. I asked for, and received from the government in Bonn, two very large volumes called the *Gedenkbuch*. They contain names, page after page after page of names, dates of birth, dates of deportation, and presumed places where these people were murdered. I looked for the names of the Berliners and where they had died - in Riga, in the Lodz ghetto, in the concentration camps.

The fourth aspect of the project was inspired by Walter Benjamin's "One-Way Street," first published in 1928. The 60 *Denkbilder*, or "sketches" that figure Benjamin's urban apocalypse became the basis for the sequence of 60 sections along the zigzagging plan of new museum building, each of which represents one of the "Stations of the Star" described in his text.

The new building is entered through the Kollegienhaus, where just inside the main entrance a void reaches from the roof of the existing Baroque building to the underground. The void contains a stair that descends beneath the existing foundations and connects to the new building above, preserving the contradictory autonomy of both and permanently binding the two together.

The descent leads to three underground axial routes, each of which tells a different story. The first and longest traces a path leading to the Stair of Continuity, then up to and through the exhibition spaces of the museum, emphasizing the continuum of history. The second leads out of the building and into the E. T. A. Hoffmann Garden of Exile and Emigration, remembering those who were forced to leave Berlin. The third leads to a dead end - the Holocaust Void. Cutting through the zigzagging plan of the new building is a void space that embodies absence, a straight line whose impenetrability becomes the central focus around which exhibitions are organized. In order to move from one side of the museum to the other, visitors must cross one of the 30 bridges that open onto this void.

The project for the museum posed questions that were relevant not only to architecture, but to all humanity. To this end, I sought to create a new architecture for a time that would reflect a new understanding of history, museums, and the relationship between program and architectural space. The work is conceived as a museum for all Berliners, for all citizens - not only those of the present, but those of the future who might find their heritage and hope in this place. With its emphasis on the Jewish dimension of Berlin's history, the building gives voice to a common fate - to the contradictions of the ordered and disordered, the chosen and not chosen, the vocal and the silent. *D.L.*

JEWISH MUSEUM BERLIN

BETWEEN THE LINES

1988, 1991–99

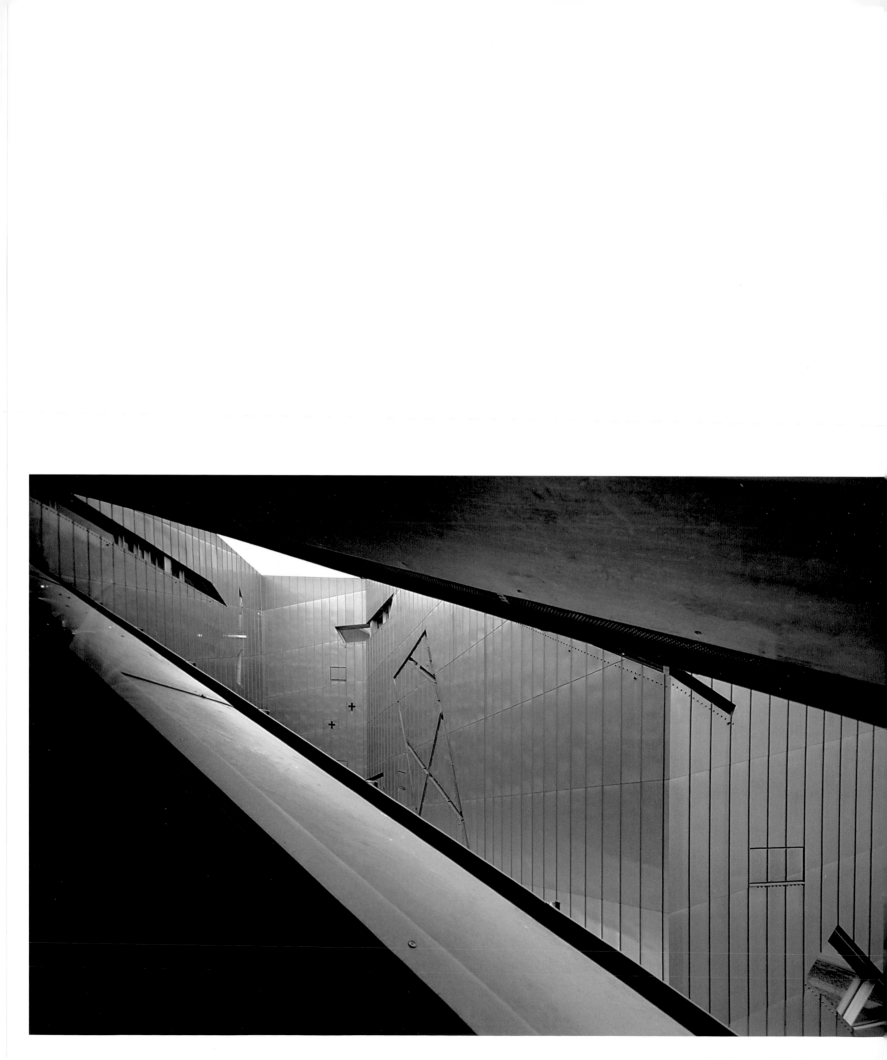

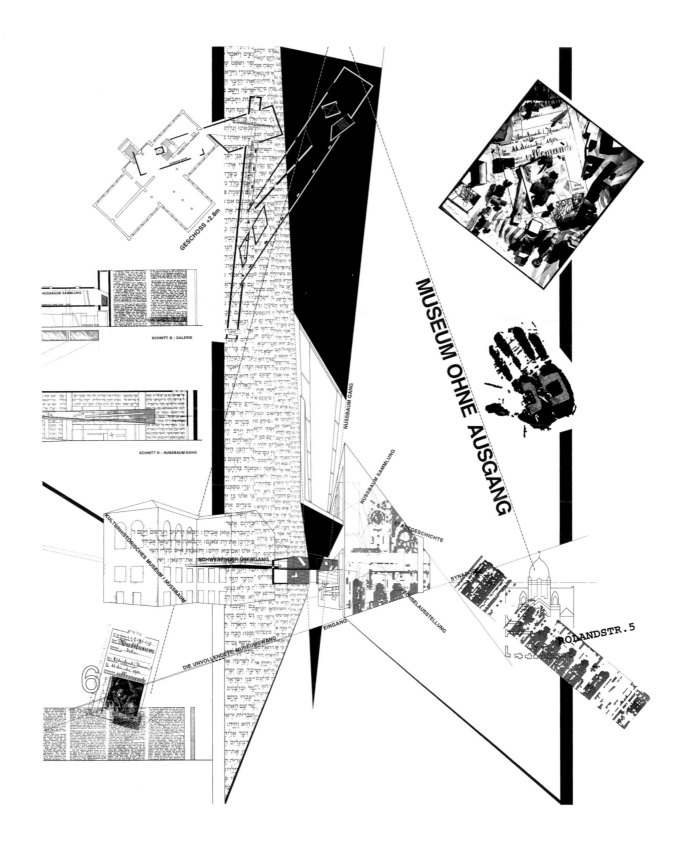

It was only by a fortuitous accident and the determined will of the town of Osnabrück that the name and work of Felix Nussbaum (1904–44) – out of millions of Jews whose names have been erased and whose lives and works have been lost forever – was elevated to public consciousness. The recovery in the early 1970s of a large number of Nussbaum's works prompted the city of Osnabrück, the artist's birthplace, to set in motion the project for a museum dedicated to his memory. It was conceived as an extension of the existing Kulturgeschichtliches Museum (Cultural History Museum) building (1888–89), which shared a site with the 1900–01 Villa Schlikker, headquarters of the Nazi Party from 1933 to 1945 – today the Haus der Erinnerung (House of Remembering), a museum of everyday life.

The task of designing a museum to house the artistic remains of Nussbaum's life raised issues that were not merely architectural, but in fact *moral*. The destruction of Jewish

MUSEUM OHNE AUSGANG / MUSEUM WITHOUT EXIT

1996–98

culture perpetuated by the Third Reich must not be dealt with solely in memorial terms. In our time, as the survivng witnesses to the annihilation of European Jewry are dying out, Nussbaum's paintings assume the status of vital documents with the power to elevate the narration of history as art and to make it emblematic of the survival of the Jewish people and European civilization. Every element of the spatial organization, geometry, and programmatic content of the scheme for the museum refers to Nussbaum's paradigmatic destiny: his early success as an artist in Berlin; the Villa Massimo fellowship to study in Rome in 1932; the tragic loss that same year of many of his paintings to a fire in his studio; the closure of the German Academy in Rome when Hitler rose to power; the consequences of Nussbaum's permanent exile from Osnabrück; the futility of escape routes through France and Belgium; and his final deportation and murder at Auschwitz. For this reason, I called it Museum ohne Ausgang, or Museum without Exit.

Nussbaum's tragic destiny can also be seen in light of his enduring belief in ultimate justice, which the scheme for the museum seeks to fulfill. It is composed of three symbolic volumes: First is the wooden building I call Nussbaum Haus, to accommodate the Nussbaum Sammlung, with galleries for the permanent collections, graphic works, archival documentation, and a large space for temporary exhibitions. Presented here are the paintings and other works that survived the fire in Nussbaum's studio. Nussbaum Haus is aligned with the site of the vanished synagogue of Osnabrück, which stood nearby on Rolandstrasse until it was burned on Kristallnacht, 1938. The Nussbaum-Gang, or Nussbaum Corridor, which cuts diagonally across the site, is a constricted, double-height, windowless concrete volume 70 meters in length, spatially conjuring Nussbaum's experience as a fugitive artist.

The long, narrow gallery is dimly lit from above by a skylight that tapers to a slit. Here are installed the paintings Nussbaum made while he lived and worked in hiding, constantly on the move to evade capture by the Nazis. Tying these two buildings together is the zinc-clad Nussbaum-Brücke, or Nussbaum Bridge. Comprising two floors of gallery space suspended above ground, it houses the lost and unidentified paintings by Nussbaum, which are gradually being recovered. The volume of the Nussbaum Bridge, entered from the Nussbaum Corridor, makes the link between past and future as it spans the gaps and hollows traced by the two other building volumes, and connects to Osnabrück's Cultural History Museum.

Visitors enter Felix-Nussbaum-Haus at one end of the Nussbaum Corridor, whose concrete exterior is a blank canvas in itself. The constricted interior

FELIX-NUSSBAUM-HAUS

space evokes a visceral sense of how Nussbaum painted during his incarcerations – a space without a horizon, which is necessary to understanding Nussbaums's oeuvre. As the corridor cuts through the building's compressed geometry, backward and forward in time, the Nussbaum Corridor becomes a visual and kinetic embodiment of his life.

In its various itineraries, with their sudden breaks, unpredictable intersections, and dead ends, the structure of the museum reflects Nussbaum's life. From the ground-floor space designated for temporary exhibitions, it is possible to glimpse the narrow vertical horizon that opens up at the end of the Nussbaum Corridor, where a stairway leads up to the second floor. The active public areas of the museum are thus left behind as one ascends to the space where Nussbaum's oeuvre unfolds. The installation on the second floor ends abruptly with Nussbaum's paintings from 1944, where the Nussbaum Bridge abuts the Cultural History Museum, signaling finality and the political futility of escape, yet it also testifies to Nussbaum's indomitable spirit, and to the resistance of art in face of inhuman oppression.

The new building does not dominate the site, but rather activates the existing ensemble of museum buildings in a crucial operation which ensures that the memory of the past will be active in the present and will participate in its ongoing narration. By virtue of its form and function, Felix-Nussbaum-Haus integrates and absorbs the Cultural History Museum and Villa Schlikker in a conscious and deliberate manner, like a transformer making the link between the town of Osnabrück and its lost history. Setting up a polyphonic composition, its three volumes act as an architectural "hinge" that holds the whole together. The museum was conceived not just as a testament to an impossible fate, but as a space of encounter between the past and the possible future. *D.L.*

The Danish Jewish Museum in Copenhagen differs from all other European Jewish museums, because Danish Jews were, by and large, saved by the deeply human response of their neighbors and compatriots in the fateful month of October 1943. In approaching this commission, I felt that the Hebrew word *mitzvah*, in its most profound, ethical meaning as a commandment, resolve, or fundamental good deed, was emblematic of the Jewish experience in Denmark, and thus *mitzvah* became the guiding light and organizing principle for the design of the museum. The site on Slotsholmen, the seat of the Danish government, and the building designated for adaptive reuse already possessed a profound historical legacy as The Royal Boat House built by King Christian IV as part of a new harbor complex in 1598. Having fallen into decline by the end of the 19th century, the building was reconstructed by Hans J. Holm between 1902 and 1906 to house the Royal Library. The building's transformations and disparate functions across almost half a millennium speak of the many layers of historical narratives that it offers to the public as a Jewish museum.

A matrix is organized by four planes that intersect in the floor structure emanating from the inside to the outside of the building, leaving their marks at the entrance of the museum and on the pedestrian path along the Royal Library Garden. The four planes, which I have called "Exodus," "Wilderness," "Giving of the Law," and "Promised Land," structure a topographical landscape that grows to its fullest density within the vaulted volume of the Royal Boat House building. These planes are articulated in both the corrugated floor sections and in the projection of walls, vitrines, and the path of the installation.

The entrance, café, and support spaces are unified by the volume of the exhibition space, which penetrates along an oblique slope that opens up a fifth virtual plane forming a surface as well as a horizon. The surface has a functional role in the installation, becoming tables, plinths, and vitrines for display. It is also a visual vector that extends the visitor's experience beyond the walls of the museum. The exhibition space is both written and read like a text within a text within a text. This is a text in which the margins —

DANISH JEWISH MUSEUM

MITZVAH
2003

On the urban level, the Danish Jewish Museum ties the old Royal Library building to the new Royal Danish Library, known as the Black Diamond (1999), and activates the pedestrian walk in the Royal Library Garden along the Proviantgården, or Royal Victualing Yard, where one of its internal planes becomes an outdoor urban space in which water and a rowboat dramatically recall the means by which the Danish Jewish community was saved. This plane draws the visitor toward the entrance in the internal courtyard of the Royal Boat House, which is marked in its horizontal as well as its vertical dimensions. On the ground plane, it is configured as an ensemble of spaces that function as intimate meeting points for visitors and an outdoor café during the summer months. The vertical walls are marked by a projection of the word *Mitzvah*, whose trace can be followed into the depths of the exhibition space.

Celebrating *mitzvah*, the museum takes the traditions of writing, reading, and memory as the basis for the matrix of the exhibition space. Thus, it is *mitzvah* itself, on the level of the emblematic as well as the architectural, that structures the dialogue between the ancient vaulted brick space of the Royal Boat House and the newly constructed wood walls of the Royal Library, creating a dynamic architectural space that offers a seamless organization of the artifacts and the path of the visitor.

walls, internal spaces, vitrines, and virtual perspectives — play a fundamental role, similar to that of the peripheral commentaries of the Talmud.

Once inside, the visitor has easy access to the café, which is also conceived of as part of the exhibition space and doubles as a projection space. Entering the exhibition proper, visitors find themselves in a space constructed entirely of wood — floors and walls — where the vitrines are reminiscent of wooden rowboats, with slightly sloping planes representing the four planes of discourse. The exhibition gallery is illuminated by light pouring in through a stained-glass window in the original building, which transforms the space as the light changes through the course of the day.

The intertwining of the old vaulted brick structure and the new volume of the exhibition space creates a dynamic dialogue between architecture of the past and that of the future. In the visitor's experience, the richness of the Jewish past in Denmark is presented as a deeply memorable and ever expanding horizon. **D.L.**

For an architect, it is always a great honor and compliment to continue working with a client to develop a building or site as it evolves. I was privileged to have a very special invitation to design an addition to the Jewish Museum Berlin, completed in 1999. Since its inauguration in 2001, the Jewish Museum's growing programs and record numbers of visitors required an expansion of the lobby and restaurant, as well as a completely new, multifunctional space for lectures, concerts, educational programs, and social events. It is a unique challenge to design an addition to your own building. After consultation with the client, I chose to locate the addition in the courtyard of the Kollegienhaus, and thus it had to work in concert with both the original building's historic facade and the zinc-clad extension that stands in contrast to it. Essentially, the new extension had to contribute to the existing dialogue between old and new.

The new structure was inspired by a form of shelter traditionally used for festive gatherings during the late-autumn Jewish holiday Sukkot, whose name derives from the Hebrew word *sukkah*, meaning "hut," and referring to the temporary structures in which the Israelites lived as they wandered the desert after escaping slavery in Egypt on their way to the Promised Land. During the seven-day Sukkot, the sukkah is used for festive meals, entertaining guests, and also resting and reflecting. An important detail is that the roof of the sukkah is left open to the sky. The joyous nature of Sukkot celebrations was the inspiration for the Glass Courtyard, programmatically invoking the communal, social, and celebratory functions of the new multipurpose space.

As a new, independent space, the luminous, transparent glass courtyard celebrates the monumentality, proportions, and beauty of the historic building, while engaging in a dynamic dialogue with the extension. The transparency allows the original Baroque building to be read clearly through the almost freestanding glass structure in the courtyard. Conversely, the faceted glass of the courtyard space reflects, reframes, and transforms the impression of the zinc-clad extension. In homage to the tradition of the sukkah being partially open to the sky, the courtyard space has a glass roof, which covers the 670-square-meter U-shaped courtyard of the Kollegienhaus. It is supported by four freestanding bundles of steel pillars resembling the structure of a tree, harking back to the tradition of using natural materials to build the sukkah. The glass facade looks onto the spacious Museum Garden. One pillar in each structural bundle is hollow and holds a sophisticated audio system equipped to handle vocal and instrumental concerts of the highest caliber. In the summer, sliding doors along the lower front elevation transform the Glass Courtyard into an open-air space where it demonstrates its social and architectural capacity to accommodate public events and occasions celebrating the meeting of German and Jewish life in the city. *D.L.*

SUKKAH
2004–07

GLASS COURTYARD

JEWISH MUSEUM BERLIN

As a Jewish architect, I am often asked if there is such a thing as a "Jewish Architecture." It is a hard question to answer. As a Jew, and as an architect, I can only say that there is certainly a Jewish sensibility, an ethic, and a humanity that resonate in my work. Perhaps what I might call the "Jewish" dimension of my work is the role that history and memory play – two features that inform all the buildings I have designed for Jewish museums in different cities around the world. As a son of Holocaust survivors, the joy and also the challenge of designing Jewish museums leave me feeling both honored and humbled. Each of the completed projects, the Jewish Museum Berlin, the Felix-Nussbaum-Haus, the Danish Jewish Museum, and now the Contemporary Jewish Museum (CJM) in San Francisco, is rooted in history and memory, but each of them communicates its particular history in a specific way. I believe that the Jewish aspect of these projects inspires architecture to contemplate questions that are relevant not only to architects, but to all humanity.

Clearly, each of my first three Jewish museums in its own way dealt directly with the tragedy and trauma of those darks times of the Holocaust: in Berlin, the history and devastation of a culture within a country: in Osnabrück, the singular horror of a rich artistic life thwarted and lost, senselessly; and in Copenhagen, the sober memory of human response to tragedy on one level, and the power of collective resistance on the other. Although all three museums were built in the shadows of the darkness of the Holocaust, in each one I tried to convey a sense of hope: the sole window in the Holocaust tower of the Jewish Museum Berlin, whose light symbolizes the hope and strength of the human heart even in the most desperate of situations; the possibility of Felix Nussbaum's voice to be heard throughout history; the reminder that, even in the darkest hour of Nazi-occupied Denmark, humanity's light shone through.

Of course, no Jewish museum can ignore the darkness of the Holocaust and the tragedies of Europe, but refracted in the light that is glimpsed in these previous projects, the CJM as an institution embodies and manifests hope. It is a beacon radiating the Jewish imagination and creativity underlying a culture of freedom, curiosity, and possibility. This museum inaugurates a dialogue that will develop in new directions in the fullness of experience: an ecumenical experience available to all those interested in the contemporary relevance – for Jews and non-Jews alike – of the 4,000-year-old "Jewish experience."

The design of the CJM in San Francisco provides space for temporary exhibitions as well as public and educational programs, and is itself a symbol dedicated to the revitalization of Jewish life in San Francisco and beyond. The building, rooted in the Jewish tradition, opens itself to the diverse contemporary currents of life and makes a fundamental contribution to the renaissance of the Yerba Buena district. The challenge, significance, and potential of this site, together with the program for the museum, are all part of the cultural process of founding an innovative Jewish institution in San Francisco that addresses identity as well as continuity.

The site, a complex urban neighborhood, provided the necessary energy for the emergence of a unique form. Housed in the abandoned late-19th-century Jessie Street Power Substation, updated in the first decade of the 20th century by Willis Polk, and landmarked in 1976, the museum literally makes visible relationships between new and old, between tradition and innovation, between the past, present, and future, bringing together 19th-, 20th-, and 21st-century architecture in one building. It will translate the physical energy associated with the legacy of the power station into the power of human communication and creativity. As the new, blue-steel-clad building is sensitively inserted in the monumental historic brick structure, the two combine and history becomes the dynamic ground for energetic transformation. Thus, history does not come to an end but opens to the future.

CONTEMPORARY JEWISH MUSEUM

L'CHAIM / TO LIFE
1998–2008

The atmosphere of the old power substation has been carefully retained and the shell of the building injected with new life as a cultural institution. At every turn, the visitor is made aware of the beauty and history of the building – the walls where batteries and equipment were once lodged, the skylights, the catwalks, and the building structure – while experiencing its transformation in counterpoint with the new building inserted within it. The new building itself synthesizes the past and the future by reinventing the historic fabric in the context of contemporary architecture. In turn, the contemporary forms are given new meaning against the backdrop of history. The CJM building is based on the Hebrew expression "L'Chaim," which means "To Life." Following the Jewish tradition, according to which letters are not mere signs, but substantial participants in the story they create, the two Hebrew letters of the chai (life) – chet and yud – with all their symbolic, mathematical, and emblematic nuance, are literally the life source that determined the form of the new museum.

The new CJM building is based on unprecedented spaces created by the two letters of the chai: the Chet provides an overall continuity for the exhibition and educational spaces, and the Yud, with its 36 windows, located on Yerba Buena Lane, gives a new identity to the Jessie Street Power Substation. Together, these letters and their meaning become a special emblem for

the ongoing development of the Yerba Buena cultural district, a symbol of the importance of culture, history, art, and community to a civilized society. Thus, the spatiality of *chai* – the fundamental emblem of Jewish life – will be experienced in a dynamic gesture responding to the many levels of interpretation the word possesses. As a matrix calling for interpretation by the visitor, the new CJM building is symbolic of the penetration of *chai* or life into the Talmudic page structure, where the margins and commentaries are as important as the central text they surround: every space in the museum is connected to the whole in an organic integration of space and function.

What we call the PaRDeS Wall greets visitors entering the museum from Jessie Square. An installation spanning the full length of the lobby, the wall is composed of built-in vitrines showcasing a sculptural abstraction of the Hebrew word *pardes*, which means a garden or orchard beyond. Each letter is embedded in the structure of the wall and illuminated, creating a dynamic effect in the central public space of the museum. PaRDeS is also an acronym in which the letters *pey*, *resh*, *dalet*, and *samech* each stand for a different layer of meaning, according to the Kabbalistic practice of identifying four distinct levels of meaning in a text: literal, allegorical, personal, and mystical. Beyond this interpretation, the PaRDeS Wall embodies the museum's philosophy of embracing multiple interpretations and meanings through its exhibitions and educational programs.

The Jewish experience presented in this discourse of forms engages the Jewish community as well as the general public with the image of a newly emerging Jewish American identity. It deals with issues of creativity, vitality, identity, and access. The spaces and their programs will delve into the depths of Jewish spirit and celebrate the discovery and relevance of Jewish culture for all. Just as the fundamental concept of the Contemporary Jewish Museum is *"L'Chaim,"* "To Life," so does the building seek to connect via the memory of the Jessie Street Power Substation with the other cultural institutions in the reenergized Yerba Buena district of San Francisco. It does so with the hope that discovery of the richness of Jewish culture will become an enduring magnet, offering the public the opportunity to share a universal heritage. *D.L.*

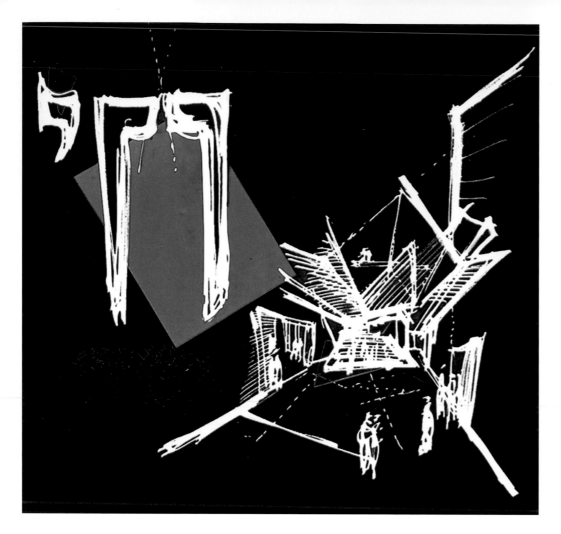

SAN FRANCISCO
JEWISH MUSEUM

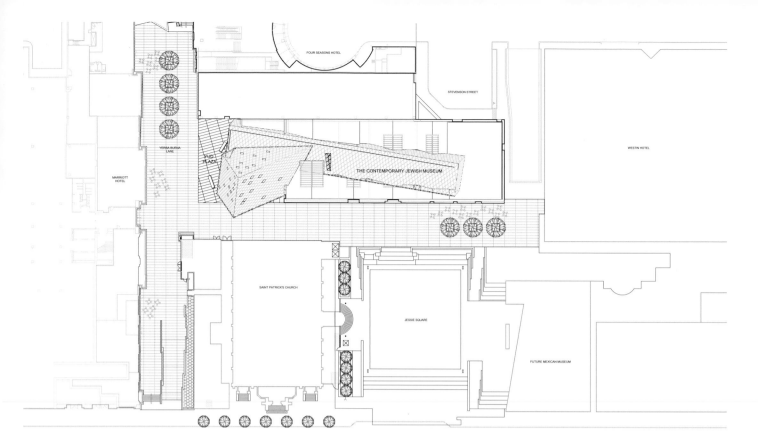

FOUR SEASONS HOTEL

STEVENSON STREET

WESTIN HOTEL

YERBA BUENA LANE

YUD PLAZA

THE CONTEMPORARY JEWISH MUSEUM

MARRIOTT HOTEL

SAINT PATRICK'S CHURCH

JESSIE SQUARE

FUTURE MEXICAN MUSEUM

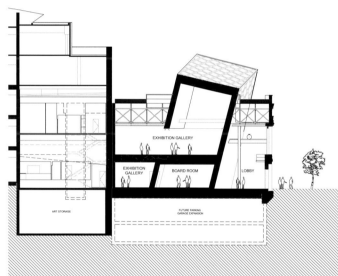

EXHIBITION GALLERY

EXHIBITION GALLERY

BOARD ROOM

LOBBY

ART STORAGE

FUTURE PARKING GARAGE EXPANSION

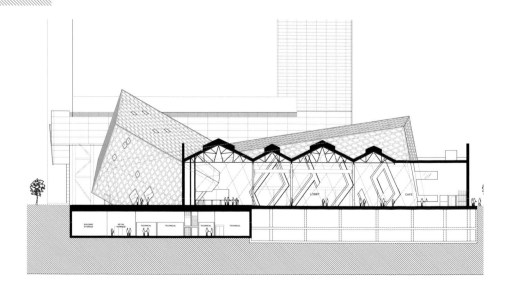

LOBBY

CAFE

BUILDING STORAGE

RETAIL STORAGE

TECHNICAL

TECHNICAL

TECHNICAL

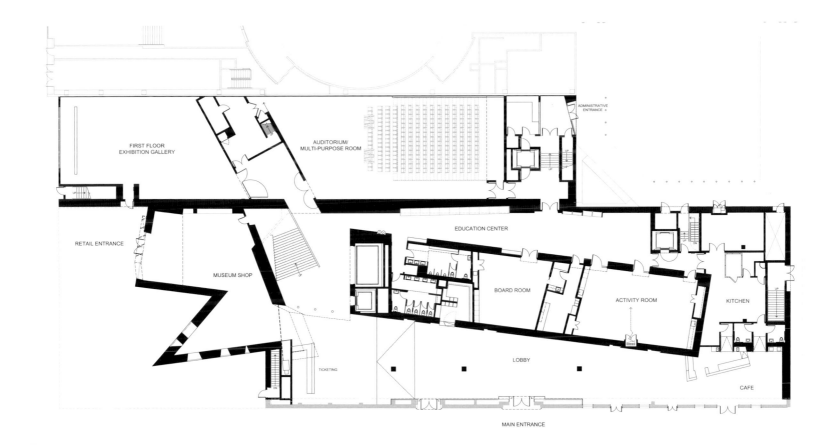

FIRST FLOOR
EXHIBITION GALLERY

AUDITORIUM/
MULTI-PURPOSE ROOM

ADMINISTRATIVE
ENTRANCE

RETAIL ENTRANCE

EDUCATION CENTER

MUSEUM SHOP

BOARD ROOM

ACTIVITY ROOM

KITCHEN

TICKETING

LOBBY

CAFE

MAIN ENTRANCE

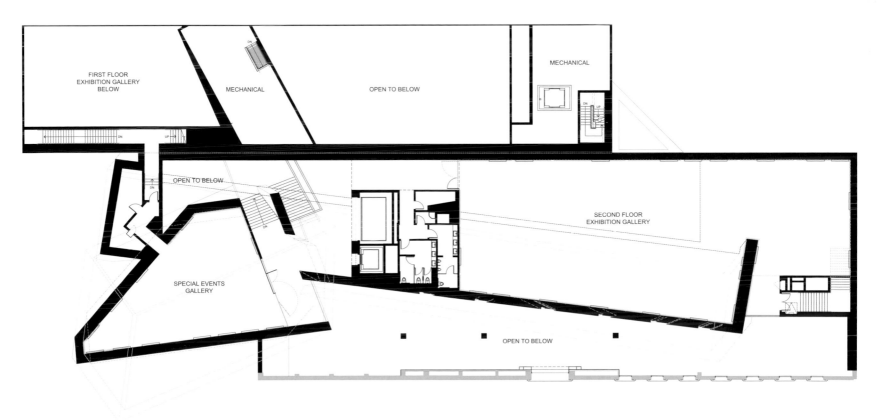

FIRST FLOOR
EXHIBITION GALLERY
BELOW

MECHANICAL

OPEN TO BELOW

MECHANICAL

OPEN TO BELOW

SECOND FLOOR
EXHIBITION GALLERY

SPECIAL EVENTS
GALLERY

OPEN TO BELOW

ABOUT DANIEL LIBESKIND

Daniel Libeskind, B.ARCH. M.A. BDA AIA, is an international figure in architectural practice and urban design. He is known for introducing a new critical discourse into architecture, and for his multidisciplinary approach. His practice extends from museums and concert halls to convention centers, universities, hotels, shopping centers, and residential projects. He also designs opera sets and maintains an object design studio. Born in Lodz, Poland, in 1946, Libeskind became an American citizen in 1965. He studied music in Israel on the America-Israel Cultural Foundation Scholarship, and continued his studies in New York, becoming a virtuoso pianist. Libeskind left music to study architecture, receiving his professional architectural degree in 1970 from the Cooper Union for the Advancement of Science and Art in New York City. He received a postgraduate degree in History and Theory of Architecture at the School of Comparative Studies, Essex University (England) in 1972. Libeskind has taught and lectured at universities around the world, and has held the Frank O. Gehry Chair at the University of Toronto, Professor at the Hochschule für Gestaltung, Karlsruhe (Germany), the Cret Chair at the University of Pennsylvania, and the Louis Kahn Chair at Yale University. He has received numerous awards, including the 2001 Hiroshima Art Prize, a prize awarded annually to an artist – but never before to an architect – whose work promotes international understanding and peace. He was awarded the 1999 Deutsche Architekturpreis (German Architecture Prize) for the Jewish Museum Berlin; the 2000 Goethe Medallion for cultural contribution; the American Academy of Arts and Letters Award for Architecture in 1996; and in the same year, the Berlin Cultural Prize. In 1990 he became a member of the European Academy of Arts and Letters. In 1997 he was awarded an Honorary Doctorate from the Humboldt Universität in Berlin; in 1999, an Honorary Doctorate from the College of Arts and Humanities, Essex University (England); in 2002, Honorary Doctorates from the University of Edinburgh and from DePaul University, Chicago; most recently, in 2004, he was awarded an Honorary Doctorate from the University of Toronto. Two of Libeskind's buildings won RIBA Awards in 2004, the London Metropolitan University Graduate Centre and the Imperial War Museum North, the latter of which was also nominated for the prestigious Stirling Prize. In the same year, Libeskind was appointed the first Cultural Ambassador for Architecture by the U.S. Department of State as part of the CultureConnect Program. Libeskind's work has been exhibited extensively in major museums and galleries around the world and has also been the subject of numerous international publications in many languages. His buildings have appeared on the covers of *Time Magazine*, *Newsweek*, *Architectural Record*, and the *Wall Street Journal*, among publications. Libeskind's ideas have influenced a new generation of architects and others interested in the future development of cities and culture. In September 2004, Riverhead Books (Penguin Group) published his memoir, *Breaking Ground: Adventures in Life and Architecture*, now available in foreign language editions reaching readers in more than 90 countries around the world.

SELECTED BIBLIOGRAPHY

Libeskind, Daniel. *Between Zero and Infinity: Selected Projects in Architecture*. New York: Rizzoli, 1981.

Libeskind, Daniel. *Chamber Works: Architectural Meditations on Themes from Heraclitus*. London: Architectural Association, 1983.

Libeskind, Daniel. *Theatrum Mundi*. London: Architectural Association, 1985.

Libeskind, Daniel. *Line of Fire*. Milan: Electa, 1988.

Hefting, Paul, and Camiel Van Winkel, eds. *Stadsmarkering. Marking the City Boundaries*, with texts by Daniel Libeskind et al. Groningen: City Planning Department, 1990.

Kristin Feireiss, ed. *Extension to the Berlin Museum with Jewish Museum*, with text by Daniel Libeskind. Berlin: Ernst & Sohn, 1992.

Libeskind, Daniel. *Countersign*. London: Academy Editions, 1991; New York: Rizzoli, 1992.

Mateus, Nuno, ed. *Daniel Libeskind – City Without a Plan: Architecture Descends into the Hexagonal Garden*. Lisbon: Blau, 1992.

Müller, Alois Martin, ed. *Radix-Matrix: Architekturen und Schriften*. Münich and New York: Prestel, 1994.

Libeskind, Daniel. *Kein Ort an seiner Stelle*. Dresden: Verlag der Künste, 1995.

El Croquis: Daniel Libeskind. Madrid, November 1996.

Libeskind, Daniel. *Radix-Matrix: Architecture and Writings*, trans. Peter Green, ed. Andrea P. A. Belloli. Münich and New York: Prestel, 1997.

Libeskind, Daniel and Cecil Balmond. *Unfolding*. Rotterdam: NAI, 1998.

Libeskind, Daniel. *Fishing from the Pavement*. Rotterdam: NAI, 1997.

Sacchi, Livio. *Daniel Libeskind: Museo ebraico, Berlino. Universale di architettura*. Turin: Testo & Immagine, 1998.

Rodiek, Thorsten. *Daniel Libeskind. Museum ohne Ausgang: Das Felix-Nussbaum-Haus des Kulturgeschichtlichen Museums Osnabrück*. Tübingen: Wasmuth, 1998.

Schneider, Bernhard. *Daniel Libeskind: Jewish Museum Berlin*, trans. John William Gabriel, with preface by Daniel Libeskind. Münich, London, and New York: Prestel, 1999.

Daniel Libeskind et al. *The Jewish Museum Berlin*. Berlin: Verlag der Kunst, 1999.

Dorner, Elke. *Das Jüdische Museum Berlin*. Berlin: Gebrüder Mann, 1999.

Libeskind, Daniel. *The Space of Encounter*. New York: Universe, 2001.

Libeskind, Daniel with Sarah Crichton. *Breaking Ground: Adventures in Life and Architecture*. London: John Murray and New York: Riverhead Books, 2004.

SELECTED WORKS

CHAMBER WORKS, CRANBROOK ACADEMY,
Bloomfield Hills, Michigan, 1983

JEWISH MUSEUM BERLIN
Berlin, Germany, 1989–99

FELIX-NUSSBAUM-HAUS
Osnabrück, Germany, 1995–98

IMPERIAL WAR MUSEUM NORTH
London, England, 1997–2002

STUDIO WEIL
Mallorca, Spain, 1998–2003

CONTEMPORARY JEWISH MUSEUM
San Francisco, California, 1998–2008

THE WOHL CENTRE
Ramat-Gan, Israel, 1999–2005

EXTENSION, DENVER ART MUSEUM
FREDERIC C. HAMILTON BUILDING,
Denver, Colorado, 2000–06

DENVER ART MUSEUM RESIDENCES
Denver, Colorado, 2000–06

WESTSIDE LEISURE AND SHOPPING CENTER
Bern, Switzerland, 2000–08

LONDON METROPOLITAN UNIVERSITY
GRADUATE CENTRE
London, England, 2001–04

MILITARY HISTORY MUSEUM
Dresden, Germany, 2001–

ROYAL ONTARIO MUSEUM
Toronto, Canada, 2002–07

CREATIVE MEDIA CENTRE
Hong Kong, China, 2002–

DANISH JEWISH MUSEUM
Copenhagen, Denmark, 2003–04

TANGENT, HYUNDAI DEVELOPMENT
CORPORATION HEADQUARTERS
Seoul, South Korea, 2003–05

MEMORY FOUNDATIONS MASTER PLAN
New York, New York, 2003–

GLASS COURTYARD, JEWISH MUSEUM BERLIN
Berlin, Germany, 2004–07

GRAND CANAL PERFORMING ARTS
CENTRE & GALLERIA
Dublin, Ireland, 2004–

MEMORIA E LUCE – 9/11 MEMORIAL
Padua, Italy, 2004–05

REFLECTIONS AT KEPPEL BAY RESIDENCES
Singapore, 2004

THE ASCENT AT ROEBLING'S BRIDGE
Covington, Kentucky, 2005–08

RETAIL COMPLEX AT MGM MIRAGE CITY CENTER
Las Vegas, Nevada, 2005–

ZLOTA 44 RESIDENCES,
Warsaw, Poland, 2005–

HAEUNDAE UDONG HYUNDAI I PARK
Busan, South Korea, 2006–

RETAIL COMPLEX AT NEW SONGDO CITY
Incheon, South Korea, 2006–

ROYAL ONTARIO MUSEUM, SPIRIT HOUSE CHAIR
Toronto, Canada, 2007

ACKNOWLEDGMENTS

If I am not for myself, who will be for me? If I am [only] for myself, what am I? And if not now, when?
Rabbi Hillel, *Pirkei Avot*

Rabbi Hillel's famous statement may have been directed to individuals, but the same principle applies to Jewish museums whose mandate is to articulate an important vision – a combination of Jewish self-expression and universal outreach – at a time when the need for culture to encourage tolerance is especially acute. This book celebrates the communities in Berlin, Osnabrück, Copenhagen, and San Francisco who invited Daniel Libeskind to create a Jewish museum that is rooted in the past and inspires a new vision for the future that embraces dialogue and intercultural exchange. It has been published to commemorate the opening of the Contemporary Jewish Museum in San Francisco.

Our exhilarating journey from the founding of the museum in 1984 to the inauguration of the new building in June 2008 bears the imprint of scores of individuals, institutions, and communities who have given generously of their time, ideas, and vision to create and sustain a museum dedicated to Jewish culture, history, art, and ideas. We salute and thank the entire community for extraordinary contributions and commitment at every level and at every stage.

We thank the many generous donors to the Campaign for the New Museum, all of whom shared in our vision to build a new museum. Our gratitude extends to the extraordinary staff who have given their expertise to make the vision come to life. We salute the Board of Trustees, each member having given generously of his or her time, ideas, and resources, and been steadfast in believing in the importance of art and ideas to build community and nourish the soul. Each Board member embraced the idea of *tzedakah* and added significantly to the many facets of the museum. Over the past five years, Roselyne Chroman Swig has served with enormous grace and integrity as the Chair of the Board of Trustees. We honor and thank her as she keeps the light shining in all of us through her spirit, passion, and values and inspires each of us to reach further, imagine more, and remain true to our vision. Alison Geballe, David Levine, and Stephen Leavitt and their families were also especially encouraging to me. I also wish to thank Clara Basile for her unwavering support and encouragement.

We are indebted to the original founders of the museum, who had the confidence to dream nearly 25 years ago to create a new kind of institution dedicated to exploring Jewish culture and wanting to share it with the broader community. In particular, we thank Alfred Fromm* and Daniel Koshland, Sr.* for their exemplary leadership and vision. We pay special tribute to the talented and dedicated former executive directors, presidents, and chairpersons who have served the institution with great care and conviction: Helene Fortgang*, Claude Ganz, F. Warren Hellman, Stephen Leavitt, Fred Levinson, Joyce Linker, Brian Lurie, Phyllis Moldaw, Bernard Osher, Linda Steinberg, and Richard L. Swig. We are grateful to the Jewish Community Federation, especially Phyllis Cook, for their support in our founding and in our development.

The remarkable new building that will capture the imagination for generations to come has been inspired by Daniel Libeskind. We thank Daniel and Nina Libeskind both for their extraordinary vision and their friendship, and for their partnership and dialogue throughout the process. Through Daniel's vision, the community has a new landmark, a new beacon for Jewish art and culture.

The extraordinary leadership of Joe Seiger as Chair of the Building Committee ensured that Daniel's vision could be realized as a building, and expertly guided the project to its successful completion. We are grateful to the team of architects, designers, builders, especially Sam Nunes, Carla Swickerath, Craig Allison, Jim Karam, and Melissa Bartolo. We thank the City of San Francisco and the San Francisco Redevelopment Agency who made it possible for us to have a role in the revitalization of the landmark Jessie Street Power Substation and the now flourishing neighborhood over which it has stood as a sentinel these many years.

We would like to thank Mitchell Schwarzer, James E. Young, and also Daniel Libeskind for their illuminating and insightful contributions to the book. Capturing this building in striking new images was no small accomplishment, and we are grateful to the photographers, especially Bruce Damonte and Mark Darley, for their inspired collaboration and engagement with the project. We greatly appreciate Rizzoli International Publications and Skira Editore for their commitment to publishing this book, especially Charles Miers, together with Maria Pia Gramaglia, Ellen Nidy, and Anthony Petrillose.

The talented and dedicated team who made this publication possible includes Mary DelMonico, who brilliantly orchestrated the many components, Denise Bratton, who thoughtfully edited the essays, and Lorraine Wild, who with Victoria Lam, so sensitively designed it. We are grateful to Richard G. Gallin for copyediting this book with such care. We also thank the team at Studio Daniel Libeskind, ably led by Carla Swickerath with the assistance of Nadine Dassain and Lynn Krogh, and Stacey Silver and her team at the Contemporary Jewish Museum for their contributions.

And finally, we thank the artists and thinkers — past, present, and future — who with their creativity, questioning, and unique perspectives are making an enduring impact on our community and our lives by inspiring us to lead a good life: one of meaning, one of thoughtfulness, and one of purpose.

Connie Wolf

*in blessed memory

CONTRIBUTORS

Mitchell Schwarzer is Chair, Department of Visual Studies, and Professor of Art History at the California College of the Arts (CCA), San Francisco. His writings focus on the history of architecture as well as urban and suburban phenomena. Among his numerous publications are *San Francisco: Architecture of the San Francisco Bay Area: History and Guide* (2006) and *Zoomscape: Architecture in Motion and Media* (2004).

Connie Wolf has been Director and CEO of the Contemporary Jewish Museum since 1999. She was Associate Director, Public Programs and Helena Rubinstein Curator of Education at the Whitney Museum of American Art, New York, 1991–99.

James E. Young is Professor of English and Judaic Studies, and Chair, Department of Judaic and Near Eastern Studies at the University of Massachusetts, Amherst, where he has taught since 1988. His publications include *At Memory's Edge: After-images of the Holocaust in Contemporary Art and Architecture* (2000), *The Texture of Memory: Holocaust Memorials and Meaning* (1994), which won the National Jewish Book Award in 1994, and *Writing and Rewriting the Holocaust: Narrative and the Consequences of Interpretation* (1990), which won a *Choice* Outstanding Academic Book Award from the American Library Association in 1988. In 1997, Young was appointed by the Berlin Senate to the five-member Findungskommission for Germany's national Memorial to the Murdered Jews of Europe, and in 2003 was invited by the Lower Manhattan Development Corporation to serve on the jury for the World Trade Center Site Memorial competition.

CAPTIONS

PHOTOGRAPH CREDITS

All images, except for the new photography of the Contemporary Jewish Museum, are provided courtesy of Studio Daniel Libeskind. Image copyright as follows:

Bitter Bredt Fotografie: back jacket, back cover, pp. 67, 69, 71, 75, 78–79, 80, 81, 84, 86–89, 90–91, 95, 96–97

Bruce Damonte: front jacket, front cover, pp. 1, 2-3, 8, 13, 14, 18, 27, 28, 29, 34, 126, 127, 128

Mark Darley: pp. 4-5, 6, 7, 9, 10, 11, 12, 15, 16-17, 19, 20, 21, 22-23, 24, 26, 25, 30

Jewish Museum Berlin; photography by Jens Ziehe: pp. 102, 103, 104-105

Stuart A. Kogod: p. 116

Michele Nastesi: pp. 72, 74, 76–77, 87

Günter Schneider (www.guenterschneider.de): pp. 64–65

T. Seidel: p. 68

Studio Daniel Libeskind: pp. 62, 82, 92, 94, 106, 108-115

BOOK CREDITS

Project Director: Mary DelMonico, Offsite: Publications, Planning, Projects

Book Design: Lorraine Wild and Victoria Lam, Green Dragon Office

Editor: Denise Bratton

Copyeditor: Richard G. Gallin

Printing and binding: CS Graphics, Singapore